CORE FOCUS

GRADE 2

TEST PRACTICE
for Common Core

Judith T. Brendel, Ed.M.
CCSS Mathematics Specialist in Curriculum and Instruction
The Madison Institute

and

Maryrose Walsh
Chester Public Schools
Chester, NJ

BARRON'S

About the Authors

Judith T. Brendel is a teacher, supervisor, author, and professional educational consultant who develops, facilitates, and presents professional learning opportunities for teachers and other educational leaders across New Jersey and nearby states. She has just completed over 35 years as a teacher and educational supervisor working in all grade-levels K–12. Presently, Judith is on the Executive Board of FEA (Foundation for Educational Administration), on the speaker's bureau of AMTNJ (Association of Math Teachers of NJ), FEA, and TMI (The Madison Institute). Judith earned a Master's Degree in Educational Administration and Curriculum and Instruction from Rutgers University and received various undergraduate degrees in mathematics, in elementary education, in art education, and earlier in fine arts from William Paterson University in New Jersey, and Hunter College in New York.

Maryrose Walsh has taught every grade-level (except first), from Montessori pre-school through Grade 8 Language Arts and Social Studies, over the last two decades. She has taught in many locations as well, including New York, Chicago, Spain, and Puerto Rico. She is currently a teacher in the Chester Consolidated School District in New Jersey. Having spent five years in 2nd grade and five years in 3rd grade, Maryrose is now moving up to 5th grade to teach ELA and Social Studies. She has earned a Master's Degree in Early Childhood Education through the College of St. Elizabeth in Morristown, New Jersey, an Advanced Certificate in Comparative European Social Studies through the University of Amsterdam in The Netherlands, and completed her undergraduate degree from St. Joseph's College in Brooklyn, New York.

All inquiries should be addressed to:
Barron's Educational Series, Inc.
250 Wireless Boulevard
Hauppauge, New York 11788
www.barronseduc.com

ISBN: 978-1-4380-0550-8
PCN: 2014946845

Date of Manufacture: December 2014
Manufactured by: B11 R11

PRINTED IN THE UNITED STATES OF AMERICA
9 8 7 6 5 4 3 2 1

CONTENTS

Note to Parents and Educators..vi

How to Use this Book...ix

Features and Benefits..x

ENGLISH LANGUAGE ARTS

Reading: Literature

Understanding Text (RL.2.1)... 2

Fables and Folktales (RL.2.2, RL.2.3)... 6

The Meaning of Words and Phrases (RL.2.4)................................... 8

Character Point of View (RL.2.6).. 12

Reading: Informational Text

Understanding Key Details (RI.2.1, RI.2.2, RI.2.3)........................ 16

Identifying the Purpose of a Text (RI.2.4, RI.2.6, RI.2.8, RI.2.9) 20

Meaning of Words and Phrases in a Text (RI.2.4, RI.2.6) 22

Comparing and Contrasting (RI.2.8, RI.2.9)................................ 24

Identifying Text Features (RI.2.5) 26

Writing

Writing Paragraphs (CCRA.W.4) 30

Writing Your Opinion (W.2.1) 32

Writing Explanatory Texts (W.2.2) 34

Writing Narrative Texts (W.2.3)... 36

Language

Collective Nouns (L.2.1.A) 38

Irregular Plural Nouns (L.2.1.B) 40

Reflexive Pronouns (L.2.1.C) 42

Adjectives and Adverbs (L.2.1.E) 44

Creating Sentences (L.2.1.F) 46

Capitalization (L.2.2.A) 48

Contractions (L.2.2.B) 50

Prefixes (L.2.4.B) 52

Suffixes (L.2.4.C) 54

Compound Words (L.2.4.D) 56

Figurative Language (L.2.5) 58

English Language Arts Practice Test 61

English Language Arts Answers Explained 77

MATH

Operations and Algebraic Thinking

Adding and Subtracting within 100 (2.OA.A.1) 88

Adding and Subtracting Fluently (2.OA.B.2) 92

Even and Odd Numbers (2.OA.C.3) 94

Using Rows and Columns (2.OA.C.4) 96

Number and Operations in Base Ten

Understanding Three-Digit Numbers (2.NBT.A.1) 98

Counting by 5s, 10s, and 100s (2.NBT.A.2) 100

Reading and Writing Numbers to 1000 (2.NBT.A.3) 104

Comparing Two Three-Digit Numbers (2.NBT.A.4) 106

Adding and Subtracting within 100 (2.NBT.B.5) 108

Adding up to Four Two-Digit Numbers (2.NBT.B.6)....................................110

Adding and Subtracting within 1000 (2.NBT.B.7) 112

Measurement and Data

Measuring (2.MD.A.1, 2.MD.A.2) 114

Measuring and Comparing (2.MD.A.3, 2.MD.A.4).......................................116

Adding and Subtracting Lengths with Nancy (2.MD.B.5) 118

Numbers, Measuring, and Number Lines (2.MD.B.6) 120

Working with Time and Money (2.MD.C.7, 2.MD.C.8) 124

Line Plots, Charts, and Tally Marks (2.MD.D.9) 128

Geometry

Shapes (2.G.A.1) 132

Rectangles and Circles (2.G.A.2, 2.G.A.3) 136

Math Practice Test 141

Math Answers Explained..155

Appendix A: Common Core Standards..177

Appendix B: Writing Rubric..182

NOTE TO PARENTS AND EDUCATORS

About Barron's Core Focus Workbooks

Barron's recognizes the need to create a product that will help students navigate the Common Core State Standards being implemented in schools across America. To meet this need, we have created grade-specific workbooks that will help bring the Common Core standards to life and ensure that students are prepared for these recently implemented assessments and expectations in learning. It is our hope that students can work through these books independently or with the guidance of a parent or teacher.

Barron's Core Focus workbooks are meant to supplement the Common Core teaching that students are receiving in their classrooms. These workbooks, all created by dedicated educators, provide specific practice on the Common Core standards through a variety of exercises and question types, including multiple choice, short answer, and extended response. The questions are organized to build on one another, increasing student understanding from one standard to the next, one step at a time, and they challenge students to apply the standards in different formats. The English Language Arts (ELA) and Math sections of the books end with a review test—this is a great way to sum up what the student has learned and reviewed from the exercises throughout.

What Is the Common Core?

"The standards are designed to be robust and relevant to the real world, reflecting the knowledge and skills that our young people need for success in college and careers."

(2012 Common Core State Standards Initiative)

Simply put, the Common Core is a series of standards that spells out exactly what students are expected to learn in English Language Arts and Mathematics throughout their years in school. These standards are fairly consistent across all grades and are designed so that students, teachers, and parents can understand what students should be learning and achieving at each grade level. Standards are organized to provide a clear understanding of the core concepts and procedures that students should master at each step of the way through school.

Unlike previous standards that were created by individual states, the Common Core is meant to be consistent throughout the country, providing all students with an equal and fair opportunity to learn English Language Arts and Math. These standards are also designed to teach students how to apply this knowledge to their everyday lives and experiences.

By sharing the same standards, states can more accurately gauge and compare students' progress and the quality of education received. The ultimate goal of the Common Core is to ensure that all students, no matter which state or part of the country they are from, will be equally ready and prepared for college and the workforce.

What Is a Standard?

A standard is a skill that should be learned by a student. Standards are organized by *domains*, which are larger groupings of related standards. For instance, in grade 2 math, there are five domains: "Operations and Algebraic Thinking," "Number and Operations in Base Ten," "Number and Operations—Fractions," "Measurement and Data," and "Geometry."

Under the domain "Operations and Algebraic Thinking," there are nine standards. These standards highlight the specific skill or understanding that a student should gain. One standard, **2.OA.A.1**, directs students "to use addition and subtraction within 100 to solve word problems involving situations of adding to, taking from, putting together, and comparing."

Note that this book does not include practice for all of the Common Core standards but only for those standards that can be utilized in the workbook format. For example, "Speaking and Listening" is not covered in this workbook. This umbrella standard, which includes "ask and answer questions about information from a speaker" (SL.2.3) and "create engaging audio recordings of stories or poems" (SL.2.5), is more interactive and would work better in a group or classroom and does not require the benefit of a workbook.

ENGLISH LANGUAGE ARTS

The English Language Arts standards are separated into different strands. The K–5 standards are comprehensive and are divided into the following areas: Reading, Writing, Speaking and Listening, Foundational Skills, and Language. The Common Core has designated separate reading standards for both fiction and nonfiction texts. These standards are identified as Reading: Literature and Reading: Informational Text. Most importantly, the reading standards emphasize engaging all students in the reading process. To meet the standards, students are expected to read multiple forms of texts, which will provide deeper literary experiences for all students. The Common Core also emphasizes the importance of text complexity. "Through extensive reading of stories, dramas, poems, and myths from diverse cultures and different time periods, students gain literary and cultural knowledge as well as familiarity with various text structures and elements." (2012 Common Core State Standards Initiative)

Each of the K–5 strands is arranged within a College and Career Readiness Anchor Standard. The Anchor Standards are the overarching goals of a K–12 curriculum. These standards remain constant in all grades. Each grade level's strands are built as scaffolds in order to achieve "official" College and Career Readiness Anchor Standards by the end of the twelfth grade. The College and Career Readiness Anchor Standards for reading literature and informational text focus on identifying key ideas and details, craft and structure, and the integration of knowledge and ideas. To meet the Common Core reading standards, students are expected to read, respond to, and interact with an array of text types of varying complexities. The College and Career Readiness Anchor Standards for writing focus on text types and purposes, production and distribution of writing, and research to build and present knowledge. To meet the Common Core writing standards, students are expected to write persuasive, narrative, and informational text. The College and Career Readiness Anchor Standards for speaking and listening focus on comprehension, collaboration, and presentation of knowledge and ideas. The speaking and listening standards focus heavily on students' ability to actively participate in groups, engage with others, and present academic information in multiple settings. The College and Career Readiness Anchor Standards for language focus on the conventions of standard English, vocabulary acquisition, and knowledge of language.

The Common Core standards are also designed to help students create digital literature and use technology to communicate ideas and knowledge. The standards are a vision of what it means to be literate in the twenty-first century. These standards foster imperative learning experiences for the twenty-first century learner. "The skills and knowledge captured in the ELA/literacy standards are designed to prepare students for life outside the classroom. They include critical-thinking skills and the ability to closely and attentively read texts in a way that will help them understand and enjoy complex works of literature." (2012 Common Core Initiative)

MATH

The Common Core mathematics standards were developed as a connected progression of learning throughout grades K–12. Ideally, this will allow teachers to close achievement gaps and give students the foundational skills necessary to continue in their learning. The Common Core provides teachers with an opportunity to build a deep and rich understanding of mathematical concepts. Instruction of Common Core mathematics standards encompasses the Mathematical Practices as well. These practices include skills that math students in every grade are expected to master. The Mathematical Practices bring rigor and rich learning opportunities to the classroom.

In grades 1 and 2, Number and Operations—Fractions is a new domain introduced to students. In grade 2, they learn to partition circles and rectangles into two, three, or four equal shares. Students learn the terms one-half, one-third, and one-fourth. Then in grade 3, there is a shift in understanding, and students are expected to understand fractions as numbers, such as ¼, and understand that this means 1 part out of 4 equal parts. The Common Core standards are related across grade levels as well as across the domains. For example, Measurement and Data standards share a number of common relationships with the Operations and Algebraic Thinking standards. This connectedness helps students prepare for the real world—remember, we do not use just one skill to balance our checkbook or determine the amount of paint for a room in our home. We have to be able to apply a variety of skills every day, and a goal of the Common Core math standards is to help prepare students for this real-life use of math. The Common Core also supports mathematical understanding of concepts that are developmentally appropriate for students. These standards allow students to build strong number sense in the early grades as they learn to count, order numbers, and compare numbers to help them think about numbers flexibly and understand the relationships between numbers as they move into the higher grades.

HOW TO USE THIS BOOK

This test practice workbook is organized by standard—one step at a time—in the order that students will likely see the concepts in the classroom. Each standard is organized in an easy-to-navigate spread(s), providing exposure to the Common Core in the simplest way possible.

In these workbooks, students will be able to build skills in multiple formats by answering multiple-choice, short-answer, and extended-response questions. Answers and explanations are included at the end of each section so students, parents, and teachers can easily assess the student's response. These explanations are a really important part of the learning process, as they provide information on the understanding needed to answer each question, common misconceptions students have, and an explanation of how students might best approach and respond to the question. Students using **Barron's Core Focus** workbooks will practice each of the specific content standards as they learn them, and also thoroughly review all of the concepts in Math or English Language Arts through the cumulative assessments.

In addition to the practice spreads covering specific standards, each section ends with a comprehensive practice test that allows students to monitor their general progress in either English Language Arts or Math. Answers and explanations provide additional guidance and instruction.

> A complete listing of all the English Language Arts and Math Common Core Standards can be found in the back of this book in Appendices A and B.

FEATURES AND BENEFITS

Barron's Core Focus workbooks provide educators, parents, and students with the opportunity to enhance their knowledge and to practice grade-level expectations within the Common Core English Language Arts and Math standards. Each workbook in this series provides questions that correlate to each standard. Every answer explanation provides helpful insight into a student's understanding, identifying common misconceptions and then providing multiple strategies. Each book also provides a cumulative assessment for each content area in Math and English Language Arts. Throughout the books, there are "Fast Fact" boxes that contain a variety of information and expose students to vocabulary, tips, and strategies.

- Parents can use these books to encourage learning at home. They can be used as guided practice or to help students with concepts they are struggling to master in school.

- Educators can use the workbooks in their classrooms to identify how to assess each standard. These books give teachers insight into what students should be able to do independently in order to master the standard. The detailed answer explanations provide opportunities for teachers to recognize misconceptions students may have about specific standards and how to successfully approach questions applicable to each standard.

- Students can use these workbooks at home to build their knowledge of English Language Arts and Math content. They can practice the content they have learned, are learning, or are going to learn. The workbooks can help prepare students for what's to come and/or as remedial practice for concepts they find challenging. The explanations in the books are extremely valuable to students as they work independently, increasing their awareness of concepts and improving their confidence as they work through each question.

> **Common Core State Standards Initiative**
> *http://www.corestandards.org/*
>
> **PARCC**
> *http://www.parcconline.org/*
>
> **Smarter Balance Assessment Consortium**
> *www.smarterbalanced.org*

ENGLISH LANGUAGE ARTS

The English Language Arts Standards are separated into different strands. The K–5 standards are comprehensive and divided into the following areas: Reading, Writing, Speaking and Listening, Foundational Skills, and Language. The Common Core has designated separate reading standards for both fiction and nonfiction texts. These standards are identified as Reading: Literature and Reading: Informational Text. In this section students will practice skills covering a variety of standards. Each section covers a specific standard found in grade 2 and provides the student with practice through multiple-choice, short-answer, matching, and extended-response questions.

UNDERSTANDING TEXT

> **RL.2.1** Ask and answer such questions as *who*, *what*, *where*, *when*, *why*, and *how* to demonstrate understanding of key details in a text.

Did you know that all reading is thinking? Well, it is! The best way to read and think at the same time is to ask and answer thinking questions like *who*, *what*, *when*, *why*, and *how* while you read.

Directions: Read the fiction passage on this page carefully. Be sure to underline words, phrases, or sentences that answer your "thinking" questions. Then, answer the multiple-choice questions on the next pages.

> Remember, you can look at the questions first and reread the passage anytime.

Excerpt from *Raccoon Rampage*
by Andrew Cope

1 *The moon was bright and everything in the forest was still. All the action was at Max's place. Rocky couldn't help but worry. "It's b-b-breaking and entering," he stuttered, pointing at the broken window. "What if the old man hears us?"*

2 *Dempsey had scarfed down so many apples that his tummy was hurting. He was prowling the top shelf in search of something that always made him feel better—muffins.*

3 *"B-but what about Max?" hissed Rocky. "We shouldn't be here, sneaking around his shop in the dead of night. He'll get upset, you know."*

Circle a letter or write your answer on the line provided.
Be sure to notice the "thinking" words in the questions.

1. *Who* is speaking in paragraph 1?
   Ⓐ   Max
   Ⓑ   Dempsey
   Ⓒ   Rocky
   Ⓓ   an old man

2. *How* do you know? Write down the word, phrase, or sentence from the passage that tells you.

   _____

   _____

3. *What* is Dempsey doing in paragraph 2?

   _____

   _____

4. *Who* is Max?
   Ⓐ   Hole-in-Tree gang member
   Ⓑ   owner
   Ⓒ   friend
   Ⓓ   raccoon

5. *How* do you know? Write down the word, phrase, or sentence from the passage that tells you.

   _____

   _____

6. *What* is Max doing?
   - Ⓐ eating
   - Ⓑ talking
   - Ⓒ sleeping
   - Ⓓ singing

7. *Where* is the story taking place?
   - Ⓐ in the forest
   - Ⓑ in a store
   - Ⓒ at Max's place
   - Ⓓ in a tree

8. *What* is the meaning of the word *scarfed* in paragraph 2?
   - Ⓐ gobbled
   - Ⓑ smiled
   - Ⓒ yelled
   - Ⓓ giggled

9. *Why* do you think Rocky and Dempsey are there? *What* makes you think so?

_____

_____

_____

_____

_____

10. In your own words, tell what this passage is about. Be sure to use words, phrases, and sentences from the passage to help.

_____

_____

_____

_____

_____

(Answers on page 77)

FABLES AND FOLKTALES

Fables are stories that teach a moral or lesson. Fables usually have animals or objects as the main characters.

Directions: Carefully read the fable below titled *The Lion and the Mouse*. Be sure to underline any words, phrases, or sentences that help you learn about the moral of the story and the characters.

The Lion and the Mouse

An Aesop Fable

*A Lion, tired with the chase, lay sleeping at full length under a shady tree. Some mice crawling over him while he slept awoke him. Laying his paw upon one of them, he was about to crush him, when the Mouse begged for mercy. "Don't hurt me, O King!" said he, "and maybe the day will come when I can be of service to you." The Lion, amused by the idea of the mouse helping him, lifted his paw and let the little creature go. Some time after, the Lion was caught in a net laid by some hunters, and, unable to free himself, made the forest shake with his roars. The Mouse, who had not been harmed by the Lion came, and with his little sharp teeth soon **gnawed** the ropes apart and set the Lion free.*

Now that you have read the fable, *The Lion and the Mouse*, answer the questions that follow. Fill in a letter or write your answer on the line provided. Be sure to notice the "thinking" words in the question. Remember, you can reread the passage any time and as often as needed.

1. *Where* does the action of the fable take place?
   (A) a backyard
   (B) a forest
   (C) a zoo
   (D) a farm

2. *How* do you know? Write down the word, phrase, or sentence that tells you.

   _____

   _____

3. *What* does the word *gnawed* mean in the last sentence?
   (A) chewed
   (B) played with
   (C) looked at
   (D) nibbled on

4. *What* is the story's moral or lesson?
   (A) One good turn deserves another.
   (B) Little friends may become great friends.
   (C) The least may help the greatest.
   (D) All of the above.

5. Compare the two main characters of the story. Explain how the Lion and the Mouse responded to their challenges in different ways.

   _____

   _____

   _____

   _____

(Answers on page 77)

THE MEANING OF WORDS AND PHRASES

> **RL.2.4** Describe how words and phrases (e.g., regular beats, alliteration, rhymes, repeated lines) supply rhythm and meaning in a story, poem, or song.

When we read poetry, we see how the poet uses words that rhyme. We also notice how a poet repeats words and phrases to create meaning. Sometimes a poet uses a tool called *alliteration* to set the mood of the poem or to describe characters and events.

> **Rhyming** is when two words sound alike even if they're spelled differently. **Alliteration** is when a few words in the sentence start with the same letter.

Directions: Read the poem and underline any rhyming words, phrases that use alliteration, or lines that are repeated. Then, answer the multiple-choice questions on the next pages. Remember, you can look at the questions first and reread the whole poem or part of the poem any time.

The Owl and the Kitty-Cat
by Edward Lear

1 The Owl and the Kitty went to sea
    In a beautiful pea-green boat,
  They took some honey, and plenty of money,
    Wrapped up in a five-pound note.
  The Owl looked up to the stars above,
    And sang to a small guitar,
  "O lovely Kitty! O Kitty, my love,
    What a beautiful Kitty you are,
        You are,
        You are!
  What a beautiful Kitty you are!"

2 Kitty said to the Owl, "You elegant fowl!
   How charmingly sweet you sing!
O let us be married! too long we have tarried:
   But what shall we do for a ring?"
They sailed away, for a year and a day,
   To the land where the Bong-Tree grows
And there in a wood a Piggy-wig stood
   With a ring at the end of his nose,
         His nose,
         His nose,
   With a ring at the end of his nose.

3 "Dear Pig, are you **willing** to sell for one shilling
   Your ring?" Said the Piggy, "I will."
So they took it away, and were married next day
   By the Turkey who lives on the hill.
They dined on mince, and slices of quince,
   Which they ate with a runcible spoon;
And hand in hand, on the edge of the sand,
   They danced by the light of the moon,
         The moon,
         The moon,
   They danced by the light of the moon.

1. *What* is this poem mostly about?
    Ⓐ   dancing in the moonlight
    Ⓑ   two animals in love
    Ⓒ   two animals in a boat
    Ⓓ   singing and playing the guitar

2. *How* do you know? Fill in all the letters below that list supporting details for what the poem is mostly about.

Ⓐ   O lovely Kitty! O Kitty my love...

Ⓑ   O let us be married, too long have we tarried...

Ⓒ   They sailed away, for a year and a day...

Ⓓ   They danced by the light of the moon...

Ⓔ   The Owl looked up to the stars above, And sang to a small guitar...

Ⓕ   So they took it away, and were married next day...

3. Are there any repeating lines in the poem?

Yes   **No**

If yes, list the repeating lines below:

_____

_____

_____

4. *Why* do you think the poet repeated these lines?

_____

_____

5. Look at the poem again. Pick out some rhyming words and write them on the lines below.

_____

_____

_____

6. *What* does the word *willing* in verse 3 mean?

Ⓐ want to

Ⓑ will not

Ⓒ would not

Ⓓ going to

(Answers on page 78)

CHARACTER POINT OF VIEW

RL.2.6 Acknowledge differences in the points of view of characters, including by speaking in a different voice for each character when reading dialogue aloud.

Directions: Read the excerpt below from *The Wizard of Oz* by L. Frank Baum. Be sure to underline any words, phrases, or sentences that help you learn about the characters. Then, answer the questions on the next page. Remember, you can look at the questions first and reread the whole passage or part of the passage at any time.

> A great way to think about your reading is to get to know the characters in the story and try to guess what they might say.

1   *When Aunt Em came there to live she was a young, pretty wife. The sun and wind had changed her, too. They had taken the sparkle from her eyes and left them a dull gray; they had taken the red from her cheeks and lips, they were gray also. She was thin and gaunt, and never smiled, now.*

2   *When Dorothy first came to her, Aunt Em had been **startled** by the child's laughter. Aunt Em would scream and press her hand upon her heart whenever Dorothy's merry voice reached her ears. She still looked at the little girl with wonder that Dorothy could find anything to laugh at.*

3   *Uncle Henry never laughed. He worked hard from morning until night and did not know what joy was. He was gray also, from his long beard to his **rough** boots. Uncle Henry looked sad and serious. He rarely spoke.*

4   *It was Toto that made Dorothy laugh, and saved her from growing gray as her Aunt Em and Uncle Henry. Toto was not gray; he was a little black dog, with long, silky hair. Toto had small black eyes that **twinkled** merrily on either side of his funny, wee nose. Toto played all day and Dorothy played with him. She loved him very much.*

1. *Who* are the characters in this passage?
   (Circle only four.)

   Aunt Em   Toto   Uncle Harry   Blackie

   Diana   Gray   Dorothy   Uncle Henry

2. Describe the character that paragraphs 1 and 2 are mostly about.
   Use the name of the character and complete sentences in
   your answer.

   _____

   _____

   _____

   _____

3. *Who* is paragraph 3 mostly about?

   _____

4. Pick an antonym (opposite) for *rough* in paragraph 3.
   - (A) brown
   - (B) striped
   - (C) bumpy
   - (D) smooth

5. Choose adjectives from the list below that might describe the
   character in paragraph 3. Fill in your choices.
   - (A) gloomy
   - (B) unhappy
   - (C) funny
   - (D) old
   - (E) sad
   - (F) tired
   - (G) excited
   - (H) happy

6. Using sentences from the passage, explain one of your adjective choices from question 5.

_____

_____

_____

_____

7. Look at paragraph 2. What do you think the word *startled* means?

   Ⓐ   surprised

   Ⓑ   saddened

   Ⓒ   suddenly

   Ⓓ   several

8. *What* character makes Dorothy happy?

_____

9. *How* does the character from question 8 make Dorothy happy?
    Be sure to use words, phrases, and/or sentences from the passage
    to explain your answer. Write in complete sentences.

    _____

    _____

    _____

    _____

    _____

10. Pick a synonym (almost the same meaning) for *twinkled* in
    paragraph 4.
    - (A)   surprised
    - (B)   sparkled
    - (C)   blinked
    - (D)   closed

(Answers on page 78)

UNDERSTANDING KEY DETAILS

RI.2.1 Ask and answer such questions as *who, what, where, when, why,* and *how* to demonstrate understanding of key details in a text.

RI.2.2 Identify the main topic of a multi-paragraph text as well as the focus of specific paragraphs within the text.

RI.2.3 Describe the connection between a series of historical events, scientific ideas or concepts, or steps in technical procedures in a text.

Directions: Read the nonfiction passage on this page carefully. Be sure to underline any words, phrases, or sentences that help you learn about the life cycle of a butterfly. Then, answer the questions on the next pages. Remember, you can look at the questions first and reread the whole passage or part of the passage any time.

> A great way to learn from your reading is to ask and answer thinking questions, such as **who**, **what**, **where**, **when**, **why**, and **how** while you read.

1   *A butterfly's life cycle has four stages. The first stage is when it is just a tiny egg. A female butterfly will lay eggs on the leaves of a plant that butterflies like to eat. The eggs look like little bubbles.*

2   *The second stage begins when the egg hatches into larva. Larva is another word for caterpillar. A caterpillar will eat and eat and eat until it is ready to **molt** or shed its skin for the next stage.*

3   *The caterpillar forms a case around itself called a chrysalis or **pupa**. It is a warm and safe place. A **metamorphosis** begins. This is the third stage of the life cycle. You cannot see inside a chrysalis, but there is a lot going on. The caterpillar is changing into a butterfly.*

4   *In the last stage, after weeks and weeks of metamorphosis, the pupa splits open and a beautiful butterfly emerges. It may take a few hours for the butterfly's wings to dry and harden, but soon after, it takes flight and is ready to begin the cycle again!*

1. *What* is this passage mostly about?
   (A) the life cycle of a caterpillar
   (B) how much caterpillar's eat
   (C) the life cycle of a butterfly
   (D) butterfly eggs

2. *How* do you know? Pick the letter below that lists a sentence that is a supporting detail for the answer to question 1.
   (A) The eggs look like little bubbles.
   (B) The caterpillar is changing into a butterfly.
   (C) A butterfly's life cycle has four stages.
   (D) A caterpillar likes to eat.

3. *What* is another name for pupa from paragraph 3?
   (A) chrysalis
   (B) sac
   (C) small bugs
   (D) pouch

4. *Why* does the caterpillar shed its skin?
   (A) It doesn't need the skin anymore.
   (B) It doesn't want the skin anymore.
   (C) The skin doesn't fit the caterpillar anymore.
   (D) The skin doesn't belong to that caterpillar.

5. *What* does the word *molt* mean? (in paragraph 2)
   (A) to grow
   (B) to melt
   (C) to shed
   (D) to sink

6. *What* happens inside the chrysalis?

   Ⓐ   The caterpillar goes to sleep.

   Ⓑ   The butterfly goes to sleep.

   Ⓒ   The caterpillar turns into a butterfly.

   Ⓓ   The butterfly turns into a caterpillar.

7. The word *metamorphosis* from paragraph 3 means?

   Ⓐ   to molt

   Ⓑ   to melt

   Ⓒ   to turn

   Ⓓ   to change

8. Which pair of words below helps to describe a chrysalis?

   Ⓐ   dark and cold

   Ⓑ   warm and safe

   Ⓒ   hangs by a tree

   Ⓓ   last stage in the butterfly life cycle

9. Which stage of a butterfly's life cycle do you think is the most important? Use the lines below to tell why.

_____

_____

10. Place a number on the line in front of each sentence below to show the order of a butterfly's life cycle.

_____ The caterpillar then makes a case called a chrysalis.

_____ The new butterfly works hard to come out of the chrysalis and soon flies away.

_____ The life of a butterfly begins in an egg.

_____ The caterpillar sheds its skin.

_____ A caterpillar likes to eat and eat and eat.

(Answers on page 79)

IDENTIFYING THE PURPOSE OF A TEXT

RI.2.4 Determine the meaning of words and phrases in a text relevant to a *grade 2 topic or subject area.*

RI.2.6 Identify the main purpose of a text, including what the author wants to answer, explain, or describe.

RI.2.8 Describe how reasons support specific points in a text.

RI.2.9 Compare and contrast the most important points presented by two texts on the same topic.

Directions: Read the nonfiction passage below about oceans. Be sure to underline any important words, phrases, or sentences. Then, answer the questions on the next page. Remember, you can look at the questions first and reread the whole passage or part of the passage any time.

A great way to learn from your reading is to ask and answer questions about what the author is trying to explain while you read. Ask yourself if the author gives you reasons why something is true.

1   The salt in the ocean comes from minerals in the earth. As rivers and glaciers travel over land, they pick up mineral salts from rocks and soil. All of the salty minerals empty into the ocean. When water **evaporates** from the ocean, the salt is left behind.

2   Over millions and millions of years, enough salt has been left behind to make the salty waters we know today. Minerals from deep inside the earth also add salt to the sea. They bubble up into the water through volcanoes and vents on the ocean floor.

3   The landscape on the ocean floor is similar to the land on the continents. The ocean floor has stretches of flat plains, canyons deeper than the Grand Canyon, mountain ranges longer than the Rocky Mountains, and volcanoes spewing hot lava. Many islands in the Pacific Ocean are actually volcanoes that poke above the water's surface.

1. *What* are the two important ideas about oceans in this passage?
   - (A) the size and location of the earth's oceans
   - (B) the saltiness of the water and size of the earth's oceans
   - (C) the location and landscape of the earth's oceans
   - (D) the landscape and saltiness of the water of the earth's oceans

2. List two reasons why the earth's oceans are salty.

   1. _____

   _____

   2. _____

   _____

3. *What* does the word *evaporates* mean in paragraph 1?
   - (A) changes from liquid form to gas form
   - (B) changes from solid form to liquid form
   - (C) changes from gas form to liquid form
   - (D) changes from liquid form to solid form

4. *How* do minerals in the earth add salt to the oceans?
   - (A) They bubble and evaporate.
   - (B) They bubble up through volcanoes and vents on the ocean floor.
   - (C) They bubble and turn into salt.
   - (D) They bubble up through ocean currents.

5. Many islands in the Pacific Ocean are really
   - (A) mountain ranges.
   - (B) volcanoes.
   - (C) flat plains.
   - (D) canyons.

(Answers on page 79)

MEANING OF WORDS AND PHRASES IN A TEXT

RI.2.4 Determine the meaning of words and phrases in a text relevant to a *grade 2 topic or subject area.*

RI.2.6 Identify the main purpose of a text including what the author wants to answer, explain, or describe.

Directions: Read the second nonfiction passage about the earth's oceans. Be sure to underline any words, phrases, or sentences that help you learn about the oceans. Then, answer the questions on the next page.

Remember, you can look at the questions first and reread the whole passage or part of the passage any time.

1 Oceans are **gigantic** pools of salty water that stretch many thousands of miles around Earth. There are five big oceans on our planet. They are the Pacific, Atlantic, Indian, Arctic, and Antarctic. To find the largest one, turn the globe until you see a side that is almost all blue. That's the Pacific Ocean. The Pacific Ocean is so big, all of the land on our planet could fit into it—with room to spare!

2 If you turn the globe to the opposite side, you'll find the Atlantic Ocean, the second-largest body of water. The next-largest ocean is located near the country of India, and it is called the Indian Ocean. The smallest ocean is the Arctic Ocean, around the North Pole. The Antarctic Ocean was just added to the world's oceans list.

3 Many smaller bodies of water—seas, lakes, rivers, bays, and gulfs—are **scattered** around our planet. And there are also giant frozen rivers, called glaciers, in the far northern and far southern areas.

1. *What* is paragraph 1 mostly about?
    A   Oceans have salty water.
    B   Oceans on other planets.
    C   It tells about the Pacific Ocean.
    D   The earth is covered by miles of oceans.

2. List the earth's oceans in order from largest to smallest.

    1. _____

    2. _____

    3. _____

    4. _____

    5. _____

3. *What* does the word *gigantic* mean in paragraph 1?
    A   huge   C   salty
    B   greasy   D   blue

4. *Where* on the earth do you find glaciers?
    A   in the East
    B   in the North
    C   in the East and West
    D   in the South and North

5. *What* does the word *scattered* mean in paragraph 3?
    A   slippery
    B   spread out
    C   sent out
    D   seen

(Answers on page 79)

23

COMPARING
AND CONTRASTING

RI.2.8 Describe how reasons support specific points in a text.

RI.2.9 Compare and contrast the most important points presented by two texts on the same topic.

Directions: You have just read two nonfiction passages about oceans. Now you are going to compare and contrast what you have learned. Reread the two passages and then answer the questions below.

Part A: How does each author describe the earth's oceans? Use details from the passages to help you answer this question. Write your answer on the lines below.

_____

_____

_____

_____

_____

_____

Part B: Use the Venn diagram to help compare and contrast the information you learned about oceans. Write key words or phrases from the passages in the correct parts of the ovals.

Oceans

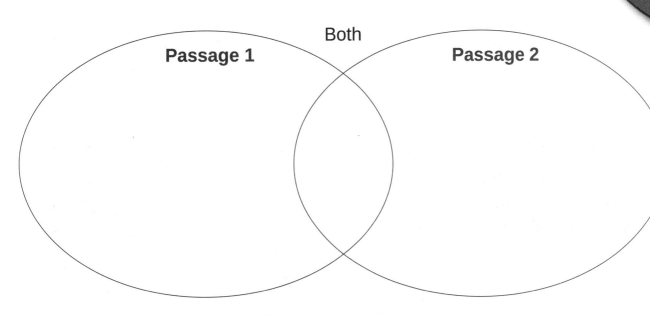

Both

Passage 1   **Passage 2**

Look at the key words and phrases you wrote in the diagram. Then write sentences on the lines below to describe what is the same about each passage and what is different.

_____

_____

_____

_____

(Answers on pages 79–80)

IDENTIFYING TEXT FEATURES

RI.2.5 Know and use text features (e.g., captions, bold print, subheadings, glossaries, indexes, electronic menus, icons) to locate key facts or information in a text efficiently.

Directions: Text features help you find information. On this page and the next, you will find boxes of different information. Look at each box and then answer the questions that follow.

You can look at the boxes of information again and again to help you answer the questions.

Text Feature A

Text Feature B

This is a koala. Although many people call this wonderful animal from Australia a bear, it is not a bear at all. Actually, it is called a marsupial because it has a pouch...just like a kangaroo!

Text Feature C

Glossary

Black Bear—smallest American bear, eats berries, has small eyes and long snout

Brown Bear—also known as Grizzly Bear

Grizzly Bear—has arms that are very strong, is omnivorous, can weigh up to 1,700 pounds

Omnivorous—an animal that eats both vegetables and meat (humans are omnivorous)

Polar Bear—world's largest predator found on land, hunts from sea ice, really good swimmer

Predator—any animal that lives by hunting and eating other animals (humans are predators)

Text Feature D

Index

Bears

  Black, 5–8

  Grizzly, 9–10

  Polar, 11–12

Climate Change, 15–16

Food, 3–4

Future, 18–19

Habitats, 1–2

Saving the Bears, 22–23

Zoos, 20–21

Text Feature E: Subheadings

Grizzly Bears	Climate Change
Zoos	Saving the Bears

1. *What* is the name of text feature B?

    _____

2. *What* pages would I read to learn about Polar Bears?

    _____

3. Write a sentence about Grizzly Bears by using one of the text features.

    _____

    _____

4. *What* is the name of the text feature you used to answer question 3?

    _____

5. Is a Koala Bear a bear? If it is not, explain what it is.

    _____

    _____

    _____

6. *What* is the name of the text feature you used to answer question 5?

    _____

7. Text Feature E lists _____ .

8. Tell why you think it is important to have subheadings in a nonfiction book.

_____

_____

_____

_____

_____

(Answers on page 80)

WRITING PARAGRAPHS

CCRA.W.4 Produce clear and coherent writing in which the development, organization, and style are appropriate to task, purpose, and audience.

A *paragraph* is a group of sentences that are about the same idea. The first sentence tells the reader the topic, or what the paragraph is about. The last sentence repeats the topic using different words to remind the reader about the paragraph they just read and provide a conclusion. The sentences in between give the reader more information about that topic. In opinion or explanatory writing, these sentences give the reader facts and details about the topic. In story writing, these sentences are full of descriptions using the five senses about the characters, setting, or plot depending on the topic of the paragraph.

> Remember to form sentences correctly, using nouns, adjectives, verbs, and adverbs!

1. You think your school needs to have gym class every day. Write a topic sentence for a paragraph that will convince your principal you are right.

   _____

   _____

2. Next, write a concluding sentence for your paragraph.

   _____

   _____

3. You're writing a paragraph all about cats. Write a topic sentence for this paragraph.

   _____

   _____

4. Next, write a concluding sentence for your paragraph all about cats.

   _____

   _____

5. You're writing a story about two friends playing baseball together. Write a topic sentence for the first paragraph of this story.

_____

_____

6. Next, write a concluding sentence for the story about the friends in question 5.

_____

_____

7. On the lines below, write a **T** for one topic sentence, **C** for one concluding sentence, or **D** for three detail sentences.
(Answers may vary.)

_____ Dogs make you happy because they wag their tails whenever they see you.

_____ Dogs are the best pet ever!

_____ There's a dog out there to become every person's dream pet.

_____ Dogs can play catch and fetch with you in the park to help you stay healthy and physically fit.

_____ Some dogs are really big, and other dogs are small enough to fit in your backpack so they can fit in any size house.

8. Now write your very own paragraph using the sentences above.

_____

_____

_____

_____

_____

_____

(Answers on page 80)

WRITING YOUR OPINION

W.2.1 Write opinion pieces in which they introduce the topic or book they are writing about, state an opinion, supply reasons that support the opinion, use linking words (e.g., because, and, also) to connect opinion and reasons, and provide a concluding statement or section.

An *opinion* is what you think about something. When you write your opinion, you must give good reasons to help your readers agree with you.

Example sentences: *I think that everybody should wear a helmet when they ride a bicycle because it is safer. Also, a helmet can protect your head and keep you from being badly hurt if you fall.*

Directions: Read the idea below that you are going to write about. Do some thinking. Then, begin writing your opinion.

Writing Idea: The principal of your school wants to buy new playground equipment to be used by the whole school during recess. She comes to your class and asks each student to write about what type of playground equipment she should buy.

Be sure to include an introduction, detailed reasons that explain your opinion, and a conclusion. Also, write in complete paragraphs.

Remember...You are writing your opinion, not telling a story. Be sure to include reasons why you think the readers should agree with you.

(Answers on page 80)

WRITING EXPLANATORY TEXTS

W.2.2 Write informative/explanatory texts in which they introduce a topic, use facts and definitions to develop points, and provide a concluding statement or section.

When you write an explanatory or informative text, you must use good facts, definitions, and descriptive examples to help your readers learn about your topic.

Example Sentences: *Snakes are interesting creatures. They slither along silently and eat small animals, like mice. Some snakes are poisonous so watch out!*

Directions: First, read the idea below that you are going to be writing about. Then, do some thinking. Make a list of everything you know about your topic. Finally, begin your writing.

> Be sure to include an introductory paragraph, detailed paragraphs with facts, definitions, and descriptions, and a concluding paragraph.

Writing Idea: Think of a person, place, or thing that you know a lot about. Write like you are an expert explaining all about your topic. Include facts and descriptions to teach your reader what you know. Some topics you might choose are a favorite vacation place, a hobby or sport you enjoy, a best friend, or a pet.

Remember, you are teaching your reader, not telling a story.

(Answers on page 80)

WRITING NARRATIVE TEXTS

> **W.2.3** Write narratives to develop real or imagined experiences or events using effective technique, descriptive details, and clear event sequences.

The last type of writing we'll practice is writing a story. A *story* is something that we read for enjoyment. A well-written story always has a beginning, middle, and an end. It also has interesting characters, realistic settings, and descriptions that help the reader create a picture in their mind.

Example sentences: *First, my friend Andy opened his present very carefully. It was wrapped in bright, green paper and had a large, silver ribbon wrapped around it. Then, he smiled with excitement. Finally, the paper was on the floor and Andy lifted the lid of the box.*

Directions: First, read the idea below that you are going to write about. Then, do some thinking. Be creative and use your imagination.

> Your story needs an introduction and conclusion, characters, setting, and events that happen in "first, next, and last order." Don't forget to use the five senses when you're writing your story.

Writing Idea: School is out for the summer. Your best friend invites you over for a play date. You walk up to your friend's front door and ring the bell. Your friend opens the door and ...

(Answers on page 80)

COLLECTIVE NOUNS

L.2.1.A Use collective nouns (e.g., group).

A noun is the name of a person, place, or thing; but they can also name groups of people, places, or things. We call these types of nouns collective nouns. Some examples of collective nouns are a **team** of players, a **pack** of cards, and a **pair** of shoes.

Directions: Choose the correct collective noun that is in bold and write it on the blank line to make the sentence correct.

1. Many _____ **(people/persons)** like to swim

    in the ocean.

2. I like to go to my _____ **(libraries/library)** to

    look for books.

3. My _____ **(class/classes)** really enjoys going

    out to play for recess.

4. Do you like to play with other _____

    (childs/children) in the park?

5. My favorite _____ **(group/groups)** of colors is

    red, blue, and yellow.

6. I think that _____ **(herds/herd)** of

   cattle is huge!

7. Which _____ **(litters/litter)** of cats

   is your favorite one?

8. Listen to the _____ **(flock/flocks)** of

   geese as they fly overhead!

9. My sister plays her flute in the best _____

   (bands/band) ever!

10. There is a very large _____ **(forest/forests)**

    of trees right behind my house.

(Answers on page 81)

39

IRREGULAR PLURAL NOUNS

> **L.2.1.B** Form and use frequently occurring irregular plural nouns (e.g., feet, children, teeth, mice, fish).

On this page, we will practice using irregular plural nouns.

An *irregular plural* noun is a noun that changes in some additional way. For example, party becomes parties, hoof becomes hooves, and man becomes men. Another type of irregular plural noun is one that doesn't change at all! For example, the plural of sheep is sheep.

> Remember, a regular plural noun is one that just adds an "s" like boy(s), girl(s), and book(s).

Directions: Choose the correct irregular plural noun in bold and write it on the blank line to make the sentence correct.

1. Most _____ **(babys/babies)** cry when they

   are hungry.

2. All of the _____ **(women/womans)** were

   waving goodbye.

3. When I am ready for bed, my mom reads me bedtime

   _____ **(storys/stories)**.

4. Do you like to play with other _____

   (families/familys) at the beach?

5. My mother cuts my food because she thinks I'm too young

to safely use _____ **(knifes/knives)**.

6. My two front _____ **(tooths/teeth)**

fell out at the same time!

7. I like to catch _____ **(mice/mouses)** in the

basement and then let them go free.

8. I helped with the _____ **(dish/dishes)**

after dinner.

9. I like to hop on one foot and jump high on two

_____ **(feet/foots)**.

10. There are many colorful _____ **(fishes/fish)**

in the ocean.

(Answers on page 81)

REFLEXIVE PRONOUNS

L.2.1.C Use reflexive pronouns (e.g., myself, ourselves).

Pronouns are words that take the place of nouns. (Example: Instead of brother use *he*, instead of sister use *she*.)

Reflexive pronouns are always partners. Look at and review the list of pronouns and their reflexive partners below. Be careful! Sometimes a reflexive pronoun partners with a noun.

> Reflexive is like the word reflection. That's what you see when you look in the mirror. So the reflexive pronoun is the reflection of the main pronoun.

Pronoun	Partner
I	myself
you	yourself
he	himself
she	herself
it	itself

Pronoun	Partner
we	ourselves
you	yourselves
they	themselves

Directions: Read each sentence carefully, then write the correct pronoun or its partner on the line. Use the word bank and the words in bold in the sentences for help.

1. **She** did her homework all by _____ .

2. **You** should buy a present for _____ .

3. **The boy** dressed _____ .

4. **We** had to walk _____ to school.

5. _____ don't like to play by **myself**.

6. **My parents** like to go to the movies by _____ .

7. Did _____ teach **yourself** how to ride

   a bicycle?

8. **The soccer team** called _____ "The Bulldogs."

9. **My grandfather** is no longer able to walk by _____ .

10. **The video game** uses a timer to turn _____ off.

(Answers on page 82)

ADJECTIVES AND ADVERBS

L.2.1.E Use adjectives and adverbs and choose between them depending on what is to be modified.

Adjectives are used to describe nouns and pronouns and adverbs are used to describe verbs. Adverbs tell *how, when,* or *where* something happens. Do you know the difference between adjectives and adverbs?

> Most adverbs have the ending *-ly.*

Directions: Read each sentence below. Underline each *-ly* word and then write either (ADJ) for adjective or (ADV) for adverb on the line at the right.

Example: *The boy cried* <u>happily</u> *when he won the race.*　　　*ADV*

1. The ugly duckling swam alone.　　　_____

2. The cat purred softly on the windowsill.　　　_____

3. The loud children entered school happily.　　　_____

4. I sadly put my toys away and went to bed.　　　_____

5. Mom filled my glass with bubbly lemonade.　　　_____

6. Stars shine brightly in the sky.   _____

7. The squiggly worm moved down the path.   _____

8. We left the room slowly at the end of the day.   _____

9. The girl gathered her curly hair in a bun.   _____

10. I shouted loudly when I won the race!   _____

(Answers on page 82)

CREATING SENTENCES

L.2.1.F Produce, expand, and rearrange complete, simple, and compound sentences.

Directions: On this page, we will practice using *adjectives*, *adverbs*, and *connecting* words to turn simple sentences into compound sentences.

Choose words from the lists below to help you grow simple sentences into compound sentences. You can also think of your own words.

Adjective	Adverbs	Connecting Words
big, blue, cheerful, happy, little, loud, old, red, short, small, soft, tall, young	always, brightly, gently, happily, high, inside, quietly, slowly, softly	and, but, or

Example: *The dog ran. (barked)*
*The **small** dog ran **quickly**.*
*The **small** dog ran **quickly**, and **barked** at the children.*

1. The cat is sleeping. (purring)

_____

_____

2. The girl played. (laughed)

_____

_____

3. The deer ran. (watched)

_____

_____

4. The boy jumped. (shouted)

_____

_____

5. The airplane flies. (lands)

_____

_____

NOW YOU TRY!

Write your own simple sentence and then a compound sentence.

Simple:

_____

_____

Compound:

_____

_____

(Answers on page 82)

47

CAPITALIZATION

L.2.2.A Capitalize holidays, product names, and geographic names.

Directions: On this page, you will find sentences with words that should be capitalized. Underline each word in the sentences that should start with a capital letter. Then rewrite the sentence correctly on the line.

REMEMBER

Proper nouns like holidays, product names, and geographic names are always capitalized.

Example: *The pacific ocean is the largest ocean on earth.*

The Pacific Ocean is the largest ocean on Earth.

1. We live on the continent of north america.

   _____

   _____

2. My favorite holiday is thanksgiving.

   _____

   _____

3. Every season is a great season in hawaii.

   _____

   _____

4. The continent across the atlantic ocean is called europe.

   _____

   _____

5. Do you like the french fries at burger barn or burger time restaurants?

_____

_____

6. The indian ocean is right near india in asia.

_____

_____

7. My favorite place to visit is Washington, d.c.

_____

_____

8. Have you ever been to madison square garden in new york city?

_____

_____

(Answers on pages 82–83)

CONTRACTIONS

L.2.2.B Use an apostrophe to form contractions and frequently occurring possessives.

Contractions are words that are shortened by leaving out a letter or letters and replacing them with an apostrophe.

In the example below, the contraction is wouldn't. It is made up of the words *would* and *not*. The apostrophe has taken the place of the letter *o*.

Example: *The boy* _wouldn't_ *wear his coat.*
would not

Directions: Read each sentence carefully. Then look at the bold words that appear under each sentence and write the contraction on the line.

1. The girl _____ write her name in cursive.
   cannot

2. Young children _____ cross the street alone.
   should not

3. He _____ want to help me clean up.
   does not

4. The people _____ watching where they were going.
   were not

5. Every time I call, _____ not home.
they are

6. _____ trying to get the attention of her student.
She is

7. Do you know why _____ shouting?
he is

8. Why _____ they waiting on the line for tickets?
are not

9. The bus _____ going in the right direction.
is not

10. Why _____ you come to my party?
did not

(Answers on page 83)

PREFIXES

L.2.4.B Determine the meaning of the new word formed when a known prefix is added to a known word (e.g., happy/unhappy, tell/retell).

A *prefix* is two or more letters added to the beginning of another word, called a base or *root word*. When you add a prefix to a root word, you change the original word's meaning because the prefix has its own meaning. Some common prefixes with their meanings are:

re-..........again or back
un-.........not
dis-.......not
pre-......before

The word *happy* means to feel good about something.

The puppy made the little girl *happy*.

Watch what happens when you add the prefix *un-* to the same word.

The little girl was *unhappy* when the puppy ran away.

The meaning of the word *happy* changed. The prefix *un-* means the opposite of. The puppy made the little girl *happy*, but when the puppy ran away, the little girl became *unhappy*.

Directions: Choose the correct prefix for the bold word and write it on the line.

Look at the list of common prefixes to help you.

*Example: My teacher told me to **re**read the story.*

1. Please _____ **lock** the door so that Grandma can come in.

2. It doesn't show good character when a person is _____ **honest**.

3. Always _____ **heat** the oven before you make brownies.

4. If you are not careful you may have to _____ **write** your paragraph.

5. _____ **tie** your shoes before you take them off.

6. It is _____ **safe** to cross the street without looking both ways.

7. I hope that my family will _____ **turn** to Disney World soon.

8. My friends and I like to watch the _____ **view** before we go to see the movie.

9. Could you _____ **tell** that funny story you told me this morning?

10. When my birthday came, I couldn't wait to _____ **wrap** my presents.

(Answers on page 83)

SUFFIXES

L.2.4.C Use a known root word as a clue to the meaning of an unknown word with the same root (e.g., addition, additional).

A *suffix* is two or more letters added to the end of a word, called a base or *root word*. When you add a suffix to a root word, you change the original word's meaning because the suffix has its own meaning. Some common suffixes with their meanings are:

-er..........person connected with skill, comparative degree

-est.......superlative degree

-ful.......full of

-less....without

Watch what happens to these words when you add the suffixes *-er* and *-est.*

Jake is *tall*. Ashley is *taller* than Jake. Sam is the *tallest* in the class.

By adding the two suffixes from above to the word *tall*, we changed its meaning two times.

Directions: Choose the correct suffix for the meaning of the sentence and write it on the line.

Example: The girl was **hope** _ful_ *that her friend could come to her party.*

> Use the list of common suffixes to help you.

1. The doctor promised that the shot would not be too **pain** _____ .

2. My **teach** _____ helps me understand double-digit addition.

3. I will be **sleep** _____ all night without my teddy bear.

4. She was the **fast** _____ runner in the race and won first place!

5. If you are **care** _____ , you will have to redo your homework.

6. It is **safe** _____ to cross the street after looking both ways.

7. Disney World was more **wonder** _____ than I ever expected!

8. This flower is the most **beaut(y)** _____ in the garden.
   (Remember what to do with the (y) before adding the suffix.)

9. Do you think that you are **smart** _____ than all of your friends?

10. When I grow up, I would like to be a **write** _____ .
    (Be careful with this one!)

(Answers on page 83)

COMPOUND WORDS

L.2.4.D Use knowledge of the meaning of individual words to predict the meaning of compound words (e.g., birdhouse, lighthouse, housefly; bookshelf, notebook, bookmark).

A *compound word* is a larger word that is made up of two smaller words. Each smaller word has its very own definition. When the two words are joined together, a larger word with a new definition is created.

Let's look at an example.

The word *rain* means water falling from the sky. The word *bow* can mean a ribbon tied in a girl's hair or the action someone takes at the end of a performance.

Watch what happens when you add rain and bow together.

**rain + bow = rainbow, a colorful arch
you see in the sky after it rains**

Directions: Choose words from the word bank below to create a compound word that matches the definition in the table on the next page.

You will use the smaller words more than once.

Word Bank

night	book	berry	house
note	side	set	time
straw	snow	shelf	shine
sun	bird	set	walk
doll	man	book	

Compound Word	Definition
1.	the rays of the sun
2.	something to write in
3.	a kind of fruit
4.	a figure made from snow
5.	a place to walk
6.	a place where birds can live
7.	a home for dolls
8.	the last light of day
9.	time of day when it is dark
10.	a place to store books

(Answers on page 83)

FIGURATIVE LANGUAGE

L.2.5 Demonstrate understanding of figurative language, word relationships, and nuances in word meanings.

L.2.5.A Identify real-life connections between words and their use (e.g., describe foods that are spicy or juicy).

L.2.5.B Distinguish shades of meaning among closely related verbs (e.g., toss, throw, hurl) and closely related adjectives (e.g., thin, slender, skinny, scrawny).

It's always important to use the best, most descriptive adjectives when you are describing something. For example—a *juicy* peach, a *salty* pretzel.

It's also important to use the best, most specific verb when you want to show exactly what is happening. For example—*toss* the Frisbee, *throw* the baseball.

Directions: Choose the most descriptive adjective (word that appears in bold) and the most specific verb to complete the sentences.

Remember to think about your choices carefully.

Examples:

She _____tossed_____ **(hurled, tossed)** *the tissue into the wastebasket.*

He ate the _____spicy_____ **(sweet, spicy)** *nachos quickly.*

1. Please _____ **(shout, speak)** quietly when you're in the library.

2. The boy _____ **(ran, tiptoed)** across the wet floor carefully.

58

3. The brownies were too _____ **(hot, heavy)**

   to eat right away.

4. I _____ **(glanced, glared)** at the clock to see

   the time.

5. She wore a _____ **(gorgeous, graceful)** blue dress

   to the party.

6. I _____ **(begged, demanded)** my parents to let me

   stay up later.

7. The man in the store _____ **(stared, glared)** at me

   angrily when I didn't pay for the water right away.

8. My friends and I think that she is as _____

   (graceful, gorgeous) as a butterfly when she dances.

9. The pitcher continued to _____ **(hurl, toss)** fastballs

   at each batter until each batter up had three strikes and the

   inning was over.

10. I really like to eat pretzels when they're _____
    (crunchy, greasy).

(Answers on pages 83–84)

ENGLISH
LANGUAGE ARTS
PRACTICE TEST

My Name: _____

Today's Date: _____

Directions: Use the passage below to answer questions 1–8.

"We shouldn't be here, sneaking around Max's shop in the dead of night," said Rocky. "Stop worrying," scolded Dempsey. "Max is sleeping. He'll never hear us, so long as we're quie—" The small raccoon brushed against a bottle. It wobbled. Dempsey gulped. He was very high up. Not good! He reached to steady the bottle and made things worse. His paws went to his eyes as the bottle fell, smashing on to the floor. All four members of the Hole-in-Tree gang froze. Dempsey peeped out from behind his claws. "Sorry!" he whispered. "Maybe Max is a heavy sleeper?" Light flooded from under a door. It was time to hide.

1. How would you describe Dempsey's behavior in the beginning of the passage?
    - (A) angry
    - (B) relaxed
    - (C) suspicious
    - (D) relieved

2. Choose the sentence that supports your answer to question 1.
    - (A) "Stop worrying," scolded Dempsey. "Max is sleeping."
    - (B) The small raccoon brushed against a bottle.
    - (C) Dempsey peeped out from behind his claws.
    - (D) He reached to steady the bottle and made things worse.

3. Which member of the gang is high up on the shelf?
    - (A) Sunshine
    - (B) Dempsey
    - (C) Rocky
    - (D) Quickpaw

4. Choose the sentence below that has a suffix in it. Underline the suffix.
   Ⓐ Max is snoring.
   Ⓑ He was up very high.
   Ⓒ All four members of the Hole-in-Tree gang froze.
   Ⓓ "Maybe Max is a heavy sleeper?"

5. The two contractions below are from the passage. Write the words that are shortened by the contractions on the lines provided. Look back at the passage and read the sentence before answering each one.

   he'll _____

   we're _____

6. Why do you think the raccoons of the Hole-in-Tree gang are hiding?
   Ⓐ They are playing a game.
   Ⓑ They are doing something wrong.
   Ⓒ They are silly.
   Ⓓ They don't like Max.

7. The Hole-in-Tree gang members are
   Ⓐ humans
   Ⓑ rats
   Ⓒ bears
   Ⓓ raccoons

8. Do you think the Hole-in-Tree gang's night raid will be a success? Use evidence from the passage to support your answer.

   _____

   _____

   _____

   _____

Directions: Use the poem below to answer questions 9–15.

The Fly
by Walter de la Mare

How large unto the tiny fly
Must little things appear!—
A rosebud like a feather bed,
*Its **prickle** like a spear;*
*A dewdrop like a **looking-glass**,*
A hair like golden wire;
The smallest grain of mustard-seed
As fierce as coals of fire;
A loaf of bread, a lofty hill;
A wasp, a cruel leopard;
And specks of salt as bright to see
As lambkins to a shepherd.

9. What is this poem mostly about?

_____

10. Give at least three examples that support your answer for question 9.

_____

_____

_____

11. In the poem, the word **dewdrop** is being compared to:
    Ⓐ binoculars.
    Ⓑ a window.
    Ⓒ a looking-glass.
    Ⓓ a reflection.

12. There are two compound words in the poem. Write each on a line below along with the two smaller words.

_____

_____

13. Choose one of the compound words and explain how combining these two smaller words has changed meaning.

_____

_____

_____

14. List at least two rhyming pairs of words.

_____

_____

15. What is another word for _prickle_ which is something that appears on the stem of a rose?
- Ⓐ horn
- Ⓑ thorn
- Ⓒ pickle
- Ⓓ pincher

The Moon
by Robert Louis Stevenson

The moon has a face like the clock in the hall;
She shines on thieves on the garden wall,
On streets and fields and harbor quays,
And birdies asleep in the forks of the trees.
The squalling cat and the squeaking mouse,
The howling dog by the door of the house,
The bat that lies in bed at noon,
All love to be out by the light of the moon.
But all of the things that belong to the day
Cuddle to sleep to be out of her way;
And flowers and children close their eyes
Till up in the morning the sun shall rise.

16. What is this poem mostly about?

_____

_____

17. Give at least three examples that support your answer for question 16.

_____

_____

_____

18. In these two lines from the poem listed below, underline the adjectives.

The squalling cat and the squeaking mouse,
The howling dog by the door of the house,...

19. Who is the poet writing about when he uses the pronoun *she* in the second verse?
(A) the clock
(B) thieves
(C) the moon
(D) a bird

20. List at least two pairs of rhyming words from the poem.

_____

_____

Directions: Read the passage below to answer questions 21–30.

Later, you will use this passage again to answer questions 33–37.

In many wetlands, cattails are the plants that grow the most easily. That's because their strong roots hold tightly to the bottoms of ponds. Their brown, long, oval-shaped tops are actually seed heads. Each seed head contains thousands of seeds. This makes it possible for each cattail to create thousands more cattail plants.

Lots of animals live in the pond water of wetlands, too. For example, crayfish live on the bottoms of ponds. Their hard shells and strong pincers help them defend themselves from predators. Their wide tails let them swim away quickly.

Other animals share ponds with crayfish. One such animal is the catfish. In most ponds of the wetland, you can see catfish swimming around in the water. They look for insects and bits of plants to eat. Their fins let them move easily through the water. They have two sharp spines on their sides for defense.

21. What is this passage mostly about?
   - (A) animals and plants living in the wetlands
   - (B) how crayfish and catfish live
   - (C) cattails and how they grow
   - (D) how animals and plants protect themselves

22. Choose a **title** for this passage.
   - (A) How Animals and Plants Protect Themselves
   - (B) Cattails and How They Grow
   - (C) Animals and Plants Living in the Wetlands
   - (D) How Crayfish and Catfish Live

23. What type of picture could you draw that would fit this passage?
    (A) a picture of a pond
    (B) a picture of a cattail plant
    (C) pictures of crayfish and catfish
    (D) all of the above

24. Where does the cattail plant store its seeds?
    (A) roots
    (B) leaves
    (C) tails
    (D) tops

25. Pick the word below that most closely matches the meaning of *predator* as it is used in the passage.
    (A) attacker
    (B) photographer
    (C) picture
    (D) follower

26. Compare how the crayfish and the catfish defend themselves.

    _____

    _____

    _____

27. List the compound words in this passage. Show the separate words for each.

    _____

    _____

28. What part of speech is the word *tightly* in the following sentence from the passage?

That's because their strong roots hold tightly *to the bottoms of ponds.*

  Ⓐ verb

  Ⓑ adverb

  Ⓒ noun

  Ⓓ adjective

29. Write the two words that make up the contraction *That's* in the following sentence from the passage on the line provided.

That's *because their strong roots hold tightly to the bottoms of ponds.*

_____

30. Summarize the passage. Include three facts you learned about the plants and animals living in the wetlands.

_____

_____

_____

_____

_____

Directions: Read the passage below to answer questions 31–40.

Remember to look back at the previous passage to answer questions 33–37.

A seahorse looks like a horse but it is really a small fish. You can find a seahorse living in shallow water in all of the Earth's oceans, except the Arctic Ocean, of course. There are many types of seahorses and, although they all look very different from one another, they do have some important things in common.

All seahorses have long snouts that look like tubes. Also, every seahorse has jaws that don't move. A seahorse has many features to help protect it from predators. Their bodies are armor-coated and they have fast-moving fins.

There are two more useful features that all seahorses have in common. One is that they are able to camouflage themselves to hide among the rocks and plants in the sea. Another feature is that each of the seahorse's eyes can move in different directions at the same time. This means that a seahorse can look for food with one eye and watch out for enemies with the other, all at the same time.

31. What is this passage mostly about?
    - (A) how seahorses protect themselves
    - (B) how seahorses look
    - (C) an introduction to what seahorses are like
    - (D) where seahorses live

32. List **three** sentences from the passage that support your answer for question 31.

    _____

    _____

    _____

Compare and contrast how crayfish, catfish, and seahorses defend themselves from predators. Write *crayfish*, *catfish*, or *seahorse* on the line provided after reading the statements below taken from one of the passages you have already read.

33. They can camouflage themselves. _____

34. They have hard shells and strong pincers. _____

35. Their eyes move in two directions. _____

36. They have sharp spines on their sides. _____

37. Their wide tails help them swim quickly. _____

38. Use the passage about seahorses you just read to create a list of words that you would expect to find in a **Glossary**.

_____

_____

_____

39. An example of a reflexive pronoun found in the passage is
    (A) themselves
    (B) himself
    (C) herself
    (D) myself

40. Write a sentence about what a seahorse can use to protect itself from a predator.

_____

Directions: Read the passage and answer questions 41–50.

Dorothy leaned her chin upon her hand and gazed thoughtfully at the scarecrow. Its head was a small sack stuffed with straw, with eyes, nose, and mouth painted on it to represent a face. An old, pointed blue hat was perched on this head, and the rest of the figure was a blue suit of clothes, worn and faded, which had also been stuffed with straw. On the feet were some old boots with blue tops just like the kind of boots every man in this place wore. The scarecrow was raised above the cornstalks by means of the pole stuck up its back.

While Dorothy was looking into the painted face of the scarecrow, she was surprised to see one of the eyes slowly wink at her. She thought she must have been mistaken at first because none of the scarecrows in Kansas ever wink. Soon, however, the figure nodded its head to her in a friendly way. Then, she climbed down from the fence and walked up to it, while Toto ran around the pole and barked.

41. Who is described in this passage?
   Ⓐ Dorothy
   Ⓑ Scarecrow
   Ⓒ Every Man
   Ⓓ Toto

42. What is the adverb in the following sentence?

   Dorothy leaned her chin upon her hand and gazed thoughtfully at the scarecrow.

   Ⓐ leaned
   Ⓑ upon
   Ⓒ gazed
   Ⓓ thoughtfully

43. What does the bold word most closely mean in the following sentence?

*Dorothy leaned her chin upon her hand and **gazed** thoughtfully at the scarecrow.*

- (A) glanced at
- (B) looked at
- (C) stared at
- (D) smiled at

44. Underline all of the adjectives you find in the following phrases.

- • small sack stuffed with straw

- • an old, pointed blue hat

- • a blue suit of clothes

- • old boots with blue tops

45. What does the bold word mean in the following sentence?

*An old, pointed blue hat was **perched** on this head.*

- (A) set down
- (B) landed
- (C) sent down
- (D) squashed

46. List compound words from the passage and show the two separate words for each.

_____

_____

47. Circle the prefix in the bold word in the sentence below. What does it mean? Fill in the correct letter.

    Its head was a small sack stuffed with straw, with eyes, nose, and mouth painted on it to **represent** *a face.*

    (A) *re-* meaning again

    (B) *rep-* meaning before

    (C) *pre-* meaning face

48. Why do the words *Kansas* and *Toto* start with capital letters?

    (A) They both begin a sentence.

    (B) They are both names of people.

    (C) They are both personal pronouns.

    (D) They are both proper nouns.

49. How would you describe Dorothy as a character in this passage?

    (A) careful

    (B) bored

    (C) curious

    (D) scared

50. Use a sentence from the text to help you explain your answer to question 49.

    _____

    _____

(Answers on pages 84–86)

ENGLISH LANGUAGE ARTS ANSWERS EXPLAINED

READING: LITERATURE

Understanding Text (RL.2.1), pages 2–5

1. **(C)** Rocky is speaking.

2. In the sentence before he speaks it says, *Rocky couldn't help but worry*.

3. Dempsey is looking for muffins. Paragraph 2 explains that muffins make Dempsey feel better.

4. **(B)** owner

5. The sentence in paragraph 1 says, *All the action was at Max's place*.

6. **(C)** sleeping

7. **(C)** at Max's place

8. **(A)** gobbled

9. Answers will vary, but should include:

   Dempsey is there because he is hungry. It says in paragraph 2 that he's eating apples. Also, he's looking for muffins to make him feel better so maybe he's also unhappy.

10. Answers will vary, but should include:

    A group of animals getting ready to break into a place for possibly food and other things. "It's b-b-breaking and entering," says one of the animals. The character named Rocky seems to be worried. He says that they shouldn't be there sneaking around the shop during the night.

Fables and Folktales (RL.2.2, RL.2.3), pages 6–7

1. **(B)** forest

   Students should choose *a forest*. Although you could see a mouse in other locations, and you would certainly see a lion in a zoo, the setting is a forest.

2. When the Lion is caught, he shakes the forest with his roars.

   Students must use textual evidence to infer the answer to this question, noticing that the lion "*made the forest shake with his roars*."

3. **(A)** chewed

4. **(D)** All of the above

   The answer is "All of the above" because all three of these lessons can be learned from the story. Although students may be confused by the phrase, "one good turn," it is important to understand that fables often teach more than one lesson. Students must also practice close reading, which means to read carefully and make connections to their own thinking experience while reading.

5. Students should show their understanding of how to compare character differences in a story. Also, they must have knowledge of the differences in the basic nature of a story's characters, which in this fable is a lion and a mouse. Of course, it is always important that students use text evidence to support their opinion.

   Sample answer: They both helped each other when they were in trouble. However, while the mouse was afraid of the lion, the lion's problem was not caused by the mouse, but by a hunter's net. Also, they asked for help in very different ways. The mouse, being weaker than the lion, begged for mercy, while the lion, who is strong and fearsome, roared his demands that he be helped. These two differences show the nature of both animals and also show that even the strong can be helped by the weak.

The Meaning of Words and Phrases (RL.2.4), pages 8–11

1. **(B)** two animals in love

2. **(A)** O lovely Kitty! O Kitty my love...

   (B) O let us be married, too long have we tarried...

   (F) So they took it away, and were married next day...

3. Yes. Students should list at least one of the following:

   *What a beautiful Kitty you are,
        You are,
        You are!
   What a beautiful Kitty you are!
   *With a ring at the end of his nose,
        His nose,
        His nose,
   With a ring at the end of his nose.
   *They danced by the light of the moon,
        The moon,
        The moon,
   They danced by the light of the moon.

4. Answers will vary. Students may mention that the repeating lines make the mood of the poem light and fun. Also, repeating the lines creates a song quality to the poem.

5. Answers will vary for question 5. The possibilities are:

   > boat – note
   > sing – ring
   > wood – stood
   > honey – money
   > married – tarried
   > willing – shilling
   > above – love
   > away – day
   > will – hill
   > Owl – fowl
   > grows – nose
   > mince – quince
   > spoon – moon
   > hand – sand

6. **(A)** want to

Character Point of View (RL.2.6), pages 12–15

1. Aunt Em, Toto, Dorothy, Uncle Henry

2. Aunt Em Answers may include: When Aunt Em was young, she was happy and her eyes sparkled. Even though she's older and doesn't smile much, Aunt Em still sees how happy Dorothy is and looks at her "with wonder." Uncle Henry is also old, but it doesn't sound like he was ever happy like Aunt Em, even when he was young. The passage says Uncle Henry looks "sad and serious."

3. Paragraph 3 is about Uncle Henry.

4. **(D)** smooth

5. **(A)** gloomy

   (B) unhappy

   (E) sad

   (F) tired

6. Uncle Henry is unhappy. Unlike Dorothy, he never laughs and rarely speaks. He also looks "sad and serious." Also, he is very tired because he works hard all day.

7. **(A)** surprised

8. Toto, her dog

9. Possible answer: I know that Toto makes Dorothy happy because it says that he made Dorothy laugh. Also, Toto played all day and Dorothy played with him. Finally, it says she loved him and when I love someone it makes me happy.

10. **(B)** sparkled

READING: INFORMATIONAL TEXT

Understanding Key Details (RI.2.1, RI.2.2, RI.2.3), pages 16–19

1. **(C)** the life cycle of a butterfly

2. **(C)** A butterfly's life cycle has four stages.

3. **(A)** chrysalis

4. **(C)** The skin doesn't fit the caterpillar anymore.

5. **(C)** to shed

6. **(C)** The caterpillar turns into a butterfly.

7. **(D)** to change

8. **(B)** warm and safe

9. Answers may vary. Some answers may include how the third stage of the butterfly's life cycle is the most important because that is when the caterpillar turns into a butterfly.

10. 4, 5, 1, 3, 2

Identifying the Purpose of a Text (RI.2.4, RI.2.6, RI.2.8, RI.2.9), pages 20–21

1. **(D)** The landscape and saltiness of the water of the earth's oceans.

2. Answers may vary. Possible answers: The salt in the ocean comes from the minerals in the earth. All of the salty minerals empty into the ocean. When water evaporates from the ocean, the salt is left behind. Minerals from deep inside the earth also bubble up into the water through volcanoes.

3. **(A)** changes from liquid form to gas form

4. **(B)** They bubble up through volcanoes and vents on the ocean floor. Salt and other minerals get left behind.

5. **(B)** Many islands in the Pacific are really volcanoes. The volcanoes can be seen above the water's surface.

Meaning of Words and Phrases in a Text (RI.2.4, RI.2.6), pages 22–23

1. **(C)** It tells about the Pacific Ocean.

2. Pacific, Atlantic, Indian, Antarctic, Arctic. By turning a globe around, it helps you see a side that is almost all blue. That is the Pacific Ocean. The second largest is the Atlantic. You can turn the globe to the other side.

3. **(A)** huge

4. **(D)** in the South and North

5. **(B)** spread out

Comparing and Contrasting (RI.2.8, RI.2.9), pages 24–25

Part A: Answers will vary but should include:

The author for the first passage tells about the salt in the ocean and what the ocean floor is like. The author of the second passage tells what oceans are, their names, and how each one is different.

Part B: Answers will vary, but should include in the Venn diagram:

Passage 1: how oceans become salty, how long it took for oceans to become salty, all about minerals, ocean floor landscapes

Both: Pacific Ocean, salt water, rivers, glaciers

Passage 2: five big oceans on our planet, size of the oceans (biggest to smallest), other bodies of water; such as bays and lakes

The passages both tell something about the Pacific Ocean and that they have salty water. Passage 1 tells about how salty oceans are. Passage 2 tells how there are five oceans and how big or small they are.

Identifying Text Features (RI.2.5), pages 26–29

1. The text feature is a caption. It describes the picture of a koala.

2. Use the **Index** to find out what page to go to, then use the **Subheading**. Pages 11 and 12 because the index tells you what pages you can start reading about polar bears.

3. Grizzly bears have arms that are very strong. They eat vegetables and meat and can weigh up to 1,700 pounds.

4. Glossary; the glossary helps to describe a grizzly bear.

5. A Koala bear is not a bear at all. It is a marsupial, just like a kangaroo, which means it has a pouch. Koalas live in Australia.

6. I used Text Feature B and that is a caption.

7. Subheadings

8. Subheadings help a reader find a main idea or topic of text.

WRITING

Writing Paragraphs (Anchor Standard CCRA.W.4), pages 30–31

Answers will vary. Below are possible student responses.

1. Children have lots of energy and the best way to use that energy is to have gym class every day we have school.

2. Children will be better able to pay attention in classes like Math and Reading if they can do physical activities every day in gym class.

3. Cats are interesting animals that are found all around the world.

4. Now you know that cats are everywhere and come in all shapes, sizes, and types.

5. We were at the park playing baseball when all of a sudden there was a really loud noise coming from the parking lot.

6. It was a relief to know that not all loud noises mean trouble.

7. D, T, C, D, D (but answers may vary.)

8. Dogs are the best pets ever! Some dogs are really big, and other dogs are small enough to fit in your backpack, so they can fit in any size house. Dogs make you happy because they wag their tails whenever they see you. Dogs can play catch and fetch with you in the park to help you stay healthy and physically fit. There's a dog out there to become every person's dream pet.

Writing Your Opinion (W.2.1) Use the simple rubric in Appendix B, page 182.

Writing Explanatory Texts (W.2.2) Use the simple rubric in Appendix B, page 182.

Writing Narrative Texts (W.2.3) Use the simple rubric in Appendix B, page 182.

LANGUAGE

Collective Nouns (L.2.1.A), pages 38–39

1. The correct answer is *people*. We use the word person if there is only one person. Students know that the use of the word many requires us to form the plural noun for person. However, we do not simply add s to person since the plural form of person is a collective noun.

2. The correct answer is *library*. We use the singular form of library because it is a collective noun.

3. The correct answer is *class*. We use the singular form of class because it is a collective noun.

4. The correct answer is *children*. We use the word child if there is only one. Students know that the use of the word other requires us to form the plural noun for child. However, we do not simply add s to child since the plural form of child is a collective noun.

5. The correct answer is *group*. We use the singular form of group because it is a collective noun.

6. The correct answer is *herd*. We use the singular form of herd because it is a collective noun.

7. The correct answer is *litter*. We use the singular form of litter because it is a collective noun.

8. The correct answer is flock. We use the singular form of flock because it is a collective noun.

9. The correct answer is *band*. We use the singular form of band because it is a collective noun.

10. The correct answer is *forest*. We use the singular form of forest because it is a collective noun.

Irregular Plural Nouns (L.2.1.B), pages 40–41

1. The correct answer is *babies*. The rule for this irregular plural noun is to change the -y to i and add -es.

2. The correct answer is *women*. This is the same change we make from the singular for man to the plural, which is, men.

3. The correct answer is *stories*. The rule for this irregular plural noun is to change the -y to *i* and add -es.

4. The correct answer is *families*. The rule for this irregular plural noun is to change the -y to *i* and *add -es.*

5. The correct answer is *knives*. The rule for this irregular plural noun is to change the *f* to v and add *s*.

6. The correct answer is *teeth*. This is an example of an irregular plural noun that changes completely when it is plural, going from one tooth to many teeth.

7. The correct answer is *mice*. This is an example of an irregular plural noun that changes completely when it is plural, going from one mouse to many mice.

8. The correct answer is *dishes*. The rule for this irregular plural is to add -es.

9. The correct answer is *feet*. This is an example of an irregular plural noun that changes completely when it is plural, going from one foot to two or more feet.

10. The correct answer is *fish*. This is an example of an irregular plural noun that does not change at all (one fish, two fish, many fish).

Reflexive Pronouns (L.2.1.C), pages 42–43

1. herself
2. yourself
3. himself
4. ourselves
5. I
6. themselves
7. you
8. themselves
9. himself
10. itself

Adjectives and Adverbs (L.2.1.E), pages 44–45

1. The ugly duckling swam alone.   ADJ
2. The cat purred softly on the windowsill.   ADV
3. The loud children entered school happily.   ADV
4. I sadly put my toys away and went to bed.   ADV
5. Mom filled my glass with bubbly lemonade.   ADJ
6. Stars shine brightly in the sky.   ADV
7. The squiggly worm moved down the path.   ADJ
8. We left the room slowly at the end of the day.   ADV
9. The girl gathered her curly hair in a bun.   ADJ
10. I shouted loudly when I won the race!   ADV

Creating Sentences (L.2.1.F), pages 46–47

Answers may vary. Some suggested student responses may include:

1. The cat is sleeping. (purring)

   The soft, white cat is sleeping. The soft, white cat is sleeping quietly. The soft, white cat is sleeping quietly and purring happily.

2. The girl played. (laughed)

   The small, young girl played. The small, young girl played inside. The small, young girl played inside and laughed happily.

3. The deer ran. (watched)

   The big, brown deer ran. The big, brown deer ran quickly. The big, brown deer ran quickly, but watched for danger.

4. The boy jumped. (shouted)

   The tall, strong boy jumped. The tall, strong boy jumped high. The tall, strong boy jumped high and shouted loudly.

5. The airplane flies. (lands)

   The giant, silver airplane flies. The giant, silver airplane flies high. The giant, silver airplane flies high and lands softly.

Now You Try!

Simple: The red balloon floated.

Compound: The big, red balloon floated gently in the sky.

Capitalization (L.2.2.A), pages 48–49

1. North America; It is the name of a continent. We live on the continent of North America.

2. Thanksgiving; It is the name of a holiday. My favorite holiday is Thanksgiving.

3. Hawaii; It is the name of a state or place. Every season is a great season in Hawaii.

4. Atlantic Ocean, Europe; Atlantic Ocean is a proper noun and Europe is the name of a country. The continent across the Atlantic Ocean is called Europe.

5. Burger Barn, Burger Time; they are both names of restaurants. Do you like the French fries at Burger Barn or Burger Time restaurants?

6. Indian Ocean, India, Asia; Indian Ocean is a proper noun and Asia is the name of a continent and country. The Indian Ocean is right near India in Asia.

7. Washington D.C. It is the name of a city/province and a proper noun. My favorite place to visit is Washington, D.C.

8. Madison Square Garden, New York City; names of places. Have you ever been to Madison Square Garden in New York City?

Contractions (L.2.2.B), pages 50–51

1. can't (cannot)
2. shouldn't (should not)
3. doesn't (does not)
4. weren't (were not)
5. they're (they are)
6. She's (she is)
7. he's (he is)
8. aren't (are not)
9. isn't (is not)
10. didn't (did not)

Prefixes (L.2.4.B), pages 52–53

1. un- (unlock) not or opposite of lock
2. dis- (dishonest) not being honest
3. pre- (preheat) before you use the oven
4. re- (rewrite) write again
5. un- (untie) not or opposite of having something tied
6. un- (unsafe) not or opposite of safe
7. re- (return) go back or return something or to someplace
8. pre- (preview) before the movie

9. re- (retell) tell again
10. un- (unwrap) opposite of wrap

Suffixes (L.2.4.C), pages 54–55

1. -ful (painful) full of pain
2. -er (teacher) person skilled in teaching or knowledge
3. -less (sleepless) without sleep
4. -est (fastest) superlative at running
5. -less (careless) without care
6. -er (safer) more safe
7. -ful (wonderful) full of wonder
8. -(i)ful (beautiful) more beautiful
9. -er (smarter) smarter than others
10. -er (writer) person skilled in writing

Compound Words (L.2.4.D), pages 56–57

Compound Word	Definition
sunshine	the rays of the sun
notebook	something to write in
strawberry	a kind of fruit
snowman	a figure made from snow
sidewalk	a place to walk
birdhouse	a place where birds can live
dollhouse	a home for dolls
sunset	the last light of day
nighttime	time of day when it is dark
bookshelf	a place to store books

Figurative Language (L.2.5), pages 58–59

1. speak; The library is a place where you speak and not shout.

2. tiptoed; You tiptoe across a wet floor so you will not slip.

83

3. hot; You will burn your mouth if you put something in your mouth that is right out of the oven.

4. glanced; You usually quickly look or glance at the time.

5. gorgeous; A dress can be gorgeous while a person can be graceful in it.

6. begged; You can beg your parents to stay up late.

7. glared; A glare on a person's face looks more angry than a stare.

8. graceful; Good dancers are graceful dancers and move with ease.

9. hurl; A hurl is more powerful than a toss. When you toss something you gently throw it.

10. crunchy; Pretzels are most often crunchy and not greasy.

English Language Arts Practice Test

1. **(B)** relaxed because he thinks that as long as they are all quiet Max will not wake up and catch them.

2. **(A)** "Stop worrying," scolded Dempsey. "Max is sleeping."

3. **(B)** Dempsey; He gulped because he was high up.

4. **(D)** "Maybe Max is a heavy sleeper?"

5. he'll = he will; we're = we are

6. **(B)** They are doing something wrong. The raccoons are trying to steal food from a shop.

7. **(D)** raccoons

8. Answers will vary, but might include how the Hole-in-Tree gang made too much noise, and woke the shop owner up, so the night raid might not have been successful.

9. Answers will vary but should include the following: The poet is looking at the world from the point of view of a fly.

10. Answers will vary. The examples are as follows: rosebud–feather bed; prickle–spear; dewdrop–looking-glass; hair–golden wire; grain of mustard-seed–coals of fire; loaf of bread–lofty hill; wasp–leopard; lambkins–shepherd.

11. **(C)** a looking-glass.

12. Dewdrop = dew + drop and rosebud = rose + bud

13. Answers will vary. Dew is the moisture that is everywhere in the morning. By adding *drop* it changes the meaning to only one small drop of dew. Rose is a flower and when bud is added, you're no longer talking about the flower. You are now referring to an earlier step in the life cycle of the rose.

14. Answers will vary. appear/spear, wire/fire, leopard/shepherd

15. **(B)** thorn; A thorn can be very sharp.

16. Answers will vary. This poem is mostly about the moon. It describes what the moon looks like and it describes its behavior (all of the things it does). The poem also talks about how people, animals, and plants behave when the moon is present.

17. Answers will vary. The examples are as follows: has a face like the clock in the hall; shines on thieves on the garden wall; shines on birdies asleep on the forks of trees; squalling cats, squeaking mice, howling dogs, the bat all love to be out by the light of the moon; things belonging to the day (flowers and children) cuddle to sleep.

18. squalling, squeaking, and howling; These words describe the actions of a cat, a mouse, and a dog.

19. **(C)** the moon

20. Answers will vary. hall/wall, mouse/house, noon/moon, day/way, eyes/rise. A correct answer may also include [quays/trees], as this is a poetic rhyming pattern. Note that

this is quite a sophisticated rhyming pair for a second grader to include in their answer.

21. **(A)** Animals and plants living in the wetlands. The author describes cattails, crayfish, and catfish.

22. **(C)** Animals and Plants Living in the Wetlands.

23. **(C)** Pictures of crayfish and catfish

24. **(D)** tops; The cattails store their seeds at their tops to create thousands more plants.

25. **(A)** attacker; Crayfish have strong pincers and wide tails to protect themselves.

26. Answers will vary. Compare: Both can swim away, the crayfish uses its wide tail and the catfish uses its fins. Contrast: The crayfish has a hard shell and strong pincers while the catfish has two sharp spines on its sides.

27. Answers will vary. Correct answers cannot be limited to including both singular and plural forms of the compound words. cattail(s) = cat + tail(s), wetland(s) = wet + lands, crayfish = cray + fish, catfish = cat + fish

28. **(B)** adverb

29. That is (writing "that" with a lower case "t" is accepted as a correct answer).

30. Answers will vary. Cattails are plants that grow well in the wetlands. Cattails grow along the edges of the ponds. Crayfish and catfish are two types of fish that live in the ponds of the wetlands. Crayfish live along the bottoms of the ponds. Catfish swim through the ponds.

31. **(C)** An introduction to what seahorses are like. The title tells readers that the passage will describe what a seahorse is, what it looks like, and how and where it lives.

32. Answers will vary. Answers should include a variety of information about seahorses, including where they live, what they look like, and how they defend themselves. Possible correct answers may include the following sentences: *A seahorse looks like a horse*

but it is really a small fish. You can find a seahorse living in shallow water in all of the earth's oceans, except the Arctic Ocean, of course. All seahorses have long snouts that look like tubes. Also, every seahorse has jaws that don't move. There are two more useful safe-keeping features that seahorses have in common. One is that they are able to camouflage themselves to hide among the rocks and plants in the sea.

33. seahorse

34. crayfish

35. seahorse

36. catfish

37. crayfish

38. Answers will vary. However, the correct answer shows the understanding that a Glossary is a list of words with their definitions. Possible correct answers may include shallow, common, features, predators, camouflage, enemies.

39. **(A)** themselves

40. Answers may vary. Seahorses can use their bodies and fast-moving fins to protect themselves from predators.

41. **(B)** Scarecrow; The first sentence describes who Dorothy is looking at, and that is the scarecrow.

42. **(D)** thoughtfully

43. **(C)** stared at; A gaze is similar to a stare.

44. small, old, pointed, blue, blue, old, blue

45. **(A)** set down; When something sets itself onto or on top of something else, it is placed, set down, or perched.

46. Note that correct answers cannot be limited to including both singular and plural forms of the compound words. However, singular or plural form of either scarecrow or cornstalk are acceptable. scarecrow(s) = scare + crow(s) **and** cornstalk(s) = corn + stalk(s)

47. **(A)** re- meaning again

48. **(D)** They are both proper nouns. Kansas is the name of a state and Toto is the name of Dorothy's dog.

49. **(C)** curious; She was interested in why a scarecrow would wink at her.

50. Answers may vary. Any of the following are acceptable, However, the bold part of the last sentence is the most accurate textual evidence. Students may respond: I know Dorothy is curious because it says in the text that... *Dorothy leaned her chin upon her hand and gazed thoughtfully at the scarecrow. While Dorothy was looking into the painted face of the scarecrow, she was surprised to see one of the eyes slowly wink at her. Soon, however, the figure nodded its head to her in a friendly way. Then,* **she climbed down from the fence and walked up to it, while Toto ran around the pole.**

MATH

The Common Core mathematics standards are designed to be building blocks between grade levels. The concepts learned in K–1 are foundational skills necessary for students to master grade 2 concepts. This allows teachers to make sure that achievement gaps are closed and that students have prior knowledge to continue their learning with more challenging concepts.

The Common Core standards in K–1 allow students to build strong number sense as they learn to count, order numbers, and compare numbers. A student's ability to think about numbers flexibly and understand the relationships between numbers is imperative to the concepts that are taught throughout all grade levels. In grade 2, students continue to have standards in Number and Operations in Base Ten, Operations and Algebraic Thinking, Measurement and Data, and Geometry. These serve as a foundational stepping stone to further learning in upcoming grade levels.

ADDING AND SUBTRACTING WITHIN 100

2.OA.A.1 Use addition and subtraction within 100 to solve one- and two-step word problems involving situations of adding to, taking from, putting together, taking apart, and comparing, with unknowns in all positions, e.g., by using drawings and equations with a symbol for the unknown number to represent the problem.

1. $25 + $40 − $4 =

   Ⓐ $69   Ⓑ $95   Ⓒ $61   Ⓓ $60

2. 65 − 5 + ☐ = 80

   Ⓐ ☐ = 5   Ⓑ ☐ = 10   Ⓒ ☐ = 15   Ⓓ ☐ = 20

3.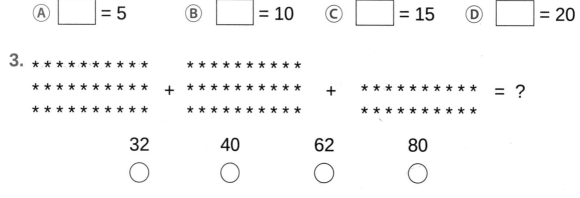

   32   40   62   80
   ○   ○   ○   ○

4. Tara has $20 and Zak has $30. How many more dollars do they need to have a total of $60?

   $50 $30 $10 $6
   ○   ○   ○   ○

5. Draw a picture to show 18 − 5 = 13

6. There are 39 crayons in the big crayon box.
   There are 12 fewer crayons in the smaller box.

   Draw a model to match this story problem.
   How many crayons are in the smaller box?　　_____ crayons

7. Eliza has 35 pennies.
   Her brother, Johnnie, gives her 20 more pennies.
   Eliza then gives 5 pennies to her little sister, Tara.
   How many pennies does Eliza have now?

   Write a number sentence to solve this problem.

   _____ ( ) _____ ( ) _____ (=) _____

8. What is true about the sum of 55 and 23?

   A. The sum is larger than 80.　　　Yes ___　　No ___

   B. The sum is smaller than 75.　　　Yes ___　　No ___

   C. The sum is 78.　　　　　　　　Yes ___　　No ___

   D. The sum is less than 90 – 5　　　Yes ___　　No ___

(Answers on pages 155–156)

PRACTICE to BECOME FLUENT
(adding and subtracting within 100)

1. 14 + 4 = ___

2. 20 + 30 = ___

3. 44 + 44 = ___

4. 50 + 8 = ___

5. 6 + 22 = ___

6. 80 + 20 = ___

7. 33 + 33 = ___

8. 7 + 90 = ___

9. 18 + 4 = ___

10. 70 + 30 = ___

11. 46 + 46 = ___

12. 6 + 26 = ___

13. ___ + 16 = 20

14. ___ + 10 = 50

15. ___ + 15 = 21

16. ___ + 6 = 96

17. 12 + ___ = 18

18. 40 + ___ = 100

19. 20 + ___ = 40

20. ___ + 2 + 3 = 10

21. ___ + 4 + 4 = 10

22. ___ + 6 + 4 = 16

23. ___ + 8 + 2 = 15

24. 25 = ___ + 15

25. 50 = ___ + 45

26. 90 = 30 + ___

27. $70 = 30 +$ _____

28. $40 +$ ___ $= 80$

29. $30 +$ ___ $= 60$

30. $25 +$ ___ $= 50$

31. $75 +$ ___ $= 100$

32. $14 - 4 =$ ___

33. $30 - 20 =$ ___

34. $44 - 22 =$ ___

35. $50 - 8 =$ ____

36. $22 - 6 =$ ___

37. $80 - 20 =$ ___

38. $33 - 11 =$ ___

39. $90 - 7 =$ ____

40. $18 - 4 =$ ____

41. $70 - 30 =$ ____

42. $46 - 36 =$ _____

43. $26 - 6 =$ _____

44. _____ $- 4 = 20$

45. _____ $- 10 = 50$

46. _____ $- 15 = 20$

47. _____ $- 5 = 95$

48. $18 -$ _____ $= 12$

49. $100 -$ _____ $= 40$

50. $40 -$ _____ $= 20$

(Answers on page 156)

ADDING AND SUBTRACTING FLUENTLY

> **2.OA.B.2** Fluently add and subtract within 20 using mental strategies. By end of grade 2, know from memory all sums of two-digit numbers.

What does *fluently* mean?

If I ask you, "What is your name?"

You answer quickly without even thinking about it.

If I ask you, "How much is **2 + 2**?"

You also answer quickly. You know the answer and this is easy for you.

$$2 + 2 = 4$$

That is what fluently means. You know the answer without even thinking.

You answer automatically.

Adding doubles is easy.

How much is **3 + 3**? That is easy. $3 + 3 = 6$

How much is **5 + 5**? That is my favorite. $5 + 5 = 10$

I also know that $10 - 5 = 5$

Adding or subtracting ones and twos is easy, too!

How much is **1 + 3**? That is easy! $1 + 3 = 4$

How much is **10 − 2**? I know that one, $10 - 2 = 8$

Adding or subtracting with 10 is a snap.

How much is **20 − 10**? Easy again, $20 - 10 = 10$

PRACTICE, PRACTICE, PRACTICE until you become fluent!

You already know so much.

Let's try some problems!

1. $10 + 9 =$ _____
   - (A) 17
   - (B) 18
   - (C) 19
   - (D) 20

2. $6 + 7 =$ _____
   - (A) 12
   - (B) 13
   - (C) 14
   - (D) 16

3. $7 + 10 =$ _____
   - (A) 71
   - (B) 17
   - (C) 18
   - (D) 3

4. $12 - 4 =$ _____
   - (A) 12
   - (B) 8
   - (C) 9
   - (D) 16

5. $8 + 10 =$ _____
   - (A) 17
   - (B) 18
   - (C) 19
   - (D) 20

6. $16 - 3 =$ _____
   - (A) 36
   - (B) 46
   - (C) 19
   - (D) 13

7. $8 + 8 =$ _____

8. $3 + 3 =$ _____

9. $6 + 6 =$ _____

10. $5 + 13 =$ _____

11. $16 - 2 =$ _____

12. $14 - 3 =$ _____

13. $7 + 7 =$ _____

14. $18 - 4 =$ _____

15. $15 - 7 =$ _____

16. $4 + 14 =$ _____

17. $9 + 9 =$ _____

18. $20 - 6 =$ _____

19. $3 + 14 =$ _____

20. $17 + 2 =$ _____

(Answers on page 156)

EVEN AND ODD NUMBERS

> **2.OA.C.3** Determine whether a group of objects (up to 20) has an odd or even number of members, e.g., by pairing objects or counting them by 2s; write an equation to express an even number as a sum of two equals.

1. Does this picture show an even or odd number of squares?

Ⓐ even   Ⓑ odd

2. Circle every two shapes.

Are there an odd or even number of shapes here? _____

3. Is this an even or odd number of triangles?

△ △ △ △ △ △ △ △ △

Ⓐ even   Ⓑ odd

How do you know?

_____

_____

4. Is the difference between these numbers even or odd?

$$9 - 4$$

Ⓐ even   Ⓑ odd

Draw a picture to show this.

5. Is the sum of 14 + 4 + 2 an even or odd number?

 Ⓐ even   Ⓑ odd

6. Write an equation to show this represents an even number.

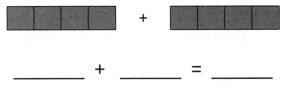

_____ + _____ = _____

10. Does this donkey have an even or an odd number of feet? Select Even or Odd.

 Ⓐ even
 Ⓑ odd

7. Are these numbers even or odd? Check Yes or No.

 A. 15 is odd   Yes __ No __

 B. 20 is odd   Yes __ No __

 C. 13 is even   Yes __ No __

 D. 6 is odd   Yes __ No __

 E. 5 is odd   Yes __ No __

11. Will these sums be even or odd? Check Even or Odd.

 A. 15 + 3   Even __ Odd __

 B. 4 + 4   Even __ Odd __

 C. 8 + 8   Even __ Odd __

 D. 7 + 8   Even __ Odd __

 E. 6 + 1   Even __ Odd __

8. Are the following numbers even or odd? Check Even or Odd.

 A. 14   Even __ Odd __

 B. 19   Even __ Odd __

 C. 9   Even __ Odd __

 D. 16   Even __ Odd __

 E. 11   Even __ Odd __

12. Circle the numbers that are odd.

   2   5   8   17

13. Is the sum of the dots an even or an odd number?

Write your answer here:

_____

(Answers on pages 156–157)

9. Write a number between 11 and 20 that is an even number.

Answer: _____

USING ROWS AND COLUMNS

> **2.OA.C.4** Use addition to find the total number of objects arranged in rectangular arrays with up to 5 rows and up to 5 columns; write an equation to express the total as a sum of equal addends.

1. How many  in all?

Ⓐ 6
Ⓑ 8
Ⓒ 9
Ⓓ 15

2. How many ✦ in all?

Ⓐ 12
Ⓑ 16
Ⓒ 20
Ⓓ 24

3. Which equation matches the picture?

Ⓐ 2 + 2 + 2 = 6
Ⓑ 1 + 5 = 6
Ⓒ 6 − 3 = 3
Ⓓ 3 + 3 = 6

4. Which equation matches the picture?

Ⓐ 2 + 2 + 2 + 2 = 8
Ⓑ 8 − 4 = 4
Ⓒ 4 + 4 = 8
Ⓓ 8 − 4 = 4

5. Write two different equations to match the picture.

```
* * * * *
* * * * *
* * * * *
```

___ (+) ___ (+) ___ = ___

___( )___( )___( )___( )___

= ___

6. Describe the array using a number sentence.

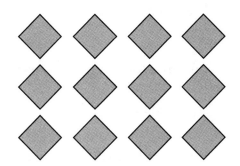

____ + ____ + ____ = ____

____ rows of _____ diamonds.

7. Circle the number sentence that matches this array?

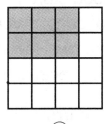

6 + 2 = 8   3 + 3 + 3 + 3 = 12

6 + 6 = 12   2 + 2 + 2 = 6

8. Shade in 2 rows of 4.

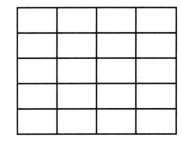

_____ + _____ = _____

9. Shade in 3 rows of 6.

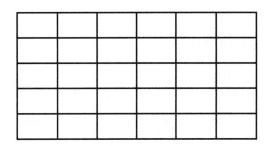

____ + ____ + ____ = _____

10. Which shading shows an array of 2 rows of 3? Circle or fill in the letter.

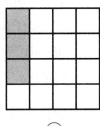 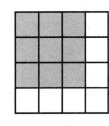 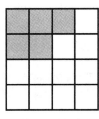

Ⓐ   Ⓑ   Ⓒ   Ⓓ

(Answers on pages 157–158)

97

UNDERSTANDING
3-DIGIT NUMBERS

2.NBT.A.1 Understand that the three digits of a three-digit number represent amounts of hundreds, tens, and ones.

1. What is the sum of **210 +** the **shaded squares** below?

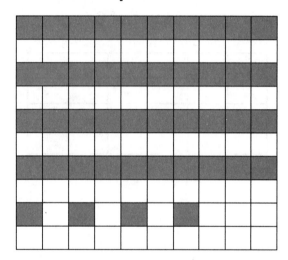

Answer: _____

2. What is the sum of all the shaded parts below?

```
100        100
```

Answer: _____

3. Add the hundreds.

Ⓐ 600 + 200 = _____
Ⓑ 100 + 300 = _____
Ⓒ 500 + 300 = _____
Ⓓ 400 + 500 = _____

4. Add

```
    5 0 0
+   1 0 0
```

5. Add

```
    7 0 0
+   2 0 0
```

6. Add

```
    3 0 0
    2 0 0
+   1 0 0
```

7. Add

```
    5 0 0
    1 0 0
+   2 0 0
```

8. The local food store received hundreds of cans of vegetables as shown below. How many cans did they receive in all?

200 cans of carrots
300 cans of corn
200 cans of peas

_____ cans in all

98

9. Show the **sum** of 324 and 563 in the number chart below.

Hundreds	Tens	Ones
+		

324 + 563 = _____

10. Show the **difference** between 438 and 305 in the number chart below.

Hundreds	Tens	Ones
−		

438 − 305 = _____

11. Which number below has 6 hundreds, 4 tens, and 3 ones?
   Ⓐ 346
   Ⓑ 436
   Ⓒ 634
   Ⓓ 643

12. Which number below is seven hundred and six?
   Ⓐ 760
   Ⓑ 706
   Ⓒ 76
   Ⓓ 076

13. How many <u>tens</u> are in the tens place in 538?

   5   3   8   0
   ◯   ◯   ◯   ◯

14. How many <u>ones</u> are in the ones place in 638?

   6   3   8   0
   ◯   ◯   ◯   ◯

15. Which place value is underlined?

   8 <u>2</u> 4

   Ⓐ ones
   Ⓑ tens
   Ⓒ hundreds

16. Circle **all** the digits that represent <u>hundreds</u>.

   340   68   743
   802   199   47

17. Write these numbers in order from smallest to largest.

   423   450   429   407   41

   ___ ___ ___ ___ ___

(Answers on pages 158–159)

99

COUNTING BY 5s, 10s, AND 100s

2.NBT.A.2 Count within 1000; skip-count by 5s, 10s, and 100s.

Sample Subtraction

Use a number line to help.

$$9 - 3 = ? \qquad 9 - 3 = 6$$

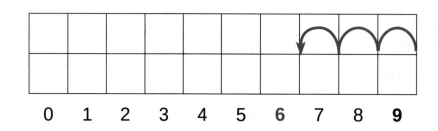

$$0 \quad 1 \quad 2 \quad 3 \quad 4 \quad 5 \quad 6 \quad 7 \quad 8 \quad 9$$

Sample Addition

Use a number line to help.

$$30 + 40 = ?$$

$$30 + 10 + 10 + 10 + 10 = 70$$

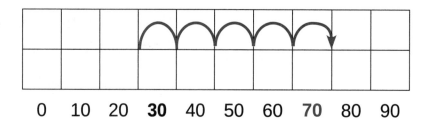

$$0 \quad 10 \quad 20 \quad 30 \quad 40 \quad 50 \quad 60 \quad 70 \quad 80 \quad 90$$

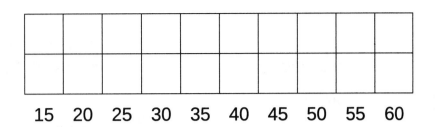

1. What two numbers are next?

25 30 35 40 ? ?

15   20   25   30   35   40   45   50   55   60

Answer: _____ and _____

2. What number is next?

60 70 80 90 ?

60	70	80	90	?

91   92   95   100
◯   ◯   ◯   ◯

3. What numbers are missing?

70 75 ___ 85 ___ 95 100

Ⓐ 76 and 77
Ⓑ 76 and 86
Ⓒ 80 and 86
Ⓓ 80 and 90

4. What numbers are missing?

65 60 ___ ___ 45 40 35

Ⓐ 59 and 49
Ⓑ 75 and 70
Ⓒ 55 and 50
Ⓓ 50 and 40

5. What number is missing?

200   300   400   ?   600

Ⓐ 401
Ⓑ 405
Ⓒ 450
Ⓓ 500

6. What number is missing?

440   540   ?   740   840

Ⓐ 542
Ⓑ 650
Ⓒ 640
Ⓓ 650

7. What is the sum of 200 + 500?

Answer: _____

8. What is the sum of 150 + 100?

Answer: _____

9. What is the difference?

850 − 200 = _____

10. What is the difference?

1000 − 300 = _____

11. Wade had 205 baseball cards. He gave 100 to his brother.

How many baseball cards does Wade have left?

Wade has _____ baseball cards left.

12. Ashley's teacher had 350 books on the library shelves. She used 50 books for her students.

How many books are still on the library shelves?

_____ books are still on the library shelves.

13. Max had 5 hits in his first ball game. He had 5 hits in his second game and 5 hits in his next game. How many hits did he have in his three games?

Max had _____ hits in his three games.

14. Shayla scored 70 points on her first math test. She scored 10 points more on her second test and 10 points more on her third test.

How much did she score on her third test?

Shayla scored _____ points on her third test.

(Answers on pages 159–160)

READING AND WRITING NUMBERS TO 1000

2.NBT.A.3 Read and write numbers to 1000 using base-ten numerals, number names, and expanded form.

1. Which number says two hundred fifty-six?
   - (A) 265
   - (B) 562
   - (C) 256
   - (D) 20056

2. Which number is equal to eight hundred twenty-five?
   - (A) 8205
   - (B) 825
   - (C) 80025
   - (D) 810025

3. 520 =
   - (A) 500 + 20
   - (B) 50 + 200
   - (C) 5 + 200
   - (D) 200 + 50

4. 605 =
   - (A) 600 + 50
   - (B) 60 + 5
   - (C) 600 + 500
   - (D) 600 + 5

5. Show the number five hundred thirty-two in the number chart below.

Hundreds	Tens	Ones

How many tens are in the number five hundred thirty-two?

Answer: _____

6. Complete the chart to show

670 + 215

Hundreds	Tens	Ones
8	8	5

Is the sum 885?

Yes___ No___

7. **Draw lines** to match the names with the numerals.

	209
Three hundred twelve	619
Two hundred ninety	312
Six hundred nineteen	942
Two hundred six	290
Nine hundred forty-two	691
	260
	206

8. **Write** the number five hundred six.

   Answer: _____

9. **Write** the number seven hundred eighty.

   Answer: _____

10. How many **tens** are in the tens place in the number 405?

    Answer: _____

11. How many **ones** are in the ones place in the number 596?

    Answer: _____

12. How many tens are in the tens place in the number 4528?

    There are _____ tens in the number above.

13. What number comes after five hundred?

    Answer: _____

    (Answers on pages 160–161)

COMPARING TWO THREE-DIGIT NUMBERS

2.NBT.A.4 Compare two three-digit numbers based on meanings of the hundreds, tens, and ones digits, using >, =, and < symbols to record the results of comparisons.

1. 890 ☐ 920

    >   =   <

3. 468 ☐ 472

    >   =   <

2. 401 ☐ 396

    >   =   <

4. 632 ☐ 629

    >   =   <

5. Fill in the blanks to make a true statement. Use the numbers 509 and 609.

   _____ > _____

6. Fill in the blanks to make a true statement. Use the numbers 950 and 910.

   _____ < _____

7. Draw a model to show which number is bigger.

   12 or 20

   Which number is bigger? _____

8. Draw a model to show which number is smaller.

   19 or 15

   Which number is smaller? _____

9. Miah has 28 cards. Ella has 19 cards.
Who has fewer cards?

_____ has fewer cards.

Explain how you know.

_____

_____

_____

10. Sydney counted 280 buttons in her grandmother's sewing box.
She counted 210 cans of paint in her grandfather's paint store.
Are there more buttons or more cans of paint?

There are more _____.

Explain how you know.

_____

_____

_____

11. Carlito says that 600 + 200 has the same value as 500 + 300.
Is he correct?

Yes _____   No _____

Explain how you know.

_____

_____

_____

(Answers on pages 161–162)

ADDING AND
SUBTRACTING WITHIN 100

2.NBT.B.5 Fluently add and subtract within 100 using strategies based on place value, properties of operations, and/or the relationship between addition and subtraction.

Sample Subtract

Tens	Ones
3	15
~~4~~	~~5~~
−	6
3	**9**

Sample Add

Tens	Ones
1	
4	9
+	6
5	**15**

Answer: 55

1.

Tens	Ones
7	3
−	8

2.

Tens	Ones
9	0
−	4

3. 75 − 16 =

4. 84 − 26 =

5.   63
      − 35

6.   34
        − 7

7.

Tens	Ones
7	4
+	8

Answer: _____

8. 35 + 6 =

Ⓐ 95

Ⓑ 40

Ⓒ 41

Ⓓ 356

9. 43 + 9 =

Ⓐ 439

Ⓑ 46

Ⓒ 50

Ⓓ 52

10. 90 − 10 + 20 =

Ⓐ 100

Ⓑ 80

Ⓒ 70

Ⓓ 60

11. Do mentally.

35 − 5 + 6 =

Ⓐ 356

Ⓑ 306

Ⓒ 360

Ⓓ 36

12. Do mentally.

46 − 3 + 10 =

Ⓐ 59

Ⓑ 56

Ⓒ 53

Ⓓ 463

13. Do mentally.

• 58 − 8 = _____

• 74 − 4 = _____

• 54 − 50 = _____

14. 100 − 98 + 2 = ____

15. 40 − 20 + 30 = ____

16. 85 − 80 + 10 = _____

17. Jeffrey had 22 mini cars, and he gave 2 to his little brother. His father then bought him 3 more. How many mini cars does Jeffrey have now?

Answer:

Jeffrey now has _____ mini cars.

18. 66 − 11 + 10 =

Answer: _____

19. Julian drove with his mom to go shopping. They drove 20 miles to one store, then 6 miles to the next store, then 26 miles home. How many miles did they drive in all?

Answer:

They drove_____ miles in all.

20. 50 + 20 − 6 =

Answer: _____

21. 12 + 12 + 12 = _____

23 + 23 + 23 = _____

22. 15 + 15 + 15 =

Answer: _____

(Answers on page 162)

ADDING UP TO FOUR TWO-DIGIT NUMBERS

2.NBT.B.6 Add up to four two-digit numbers using strategies based on place value and properties of operations.

1. Desiree loves to read. She has 12 books about animals. She also has 14 mystery books and 15 books about different countries. How many books does she have in all?

   31   39   41   42
   ○   ○   ○   ○

2. Desiree also likes to shop. She went shopping with her mother for a party. They bought 24 paper plates, 18 paper cups, and 12 cans of juice. How many items did they buy in all?

   44   48   53   54
   ○   ○   ○   ○

3. $30 + 45 + 20 =$

   77   95   105   140
   ○   ○   ○   ○

4. $20 + 14 + 20 + 14 =$

   56   58   68   70
   ○   ○   ○   ○

5. Eliza says it is easy to add these four numbers.

   $20 + 12 + 30 + 7$

   Why are they easy to add?

   _____

   _____

   What is the sum of these

   numbers? _____

6. Eliza's brother, Johnnie, says some numbers are easy to add and some are not. He says it is easy to add

   $13 + 41 + 11 + 43$

   Why are they easy to add?

   _____

   _____

   _____

   What is their sum? _____

7. Johnnie says it is harder to add

   56 + 66 + 33 + 23

   Why are they harder to add?

   _____

   _____

   What is their sum? _____

8. Johnnie's teacher has
   16 yellow balloons, 24 red
   balloons, and 18 blue ones.
   How many balloons does she
   have in all?

   Johnnie's teacher has _____
   balloons in all.

9. His school has 64 big windows
   and 38 small windows. How
   many windows does the school
   have?

   The school has _____
   windows in all.

10. In the spring Eliza
    went to the zoo with
    Johnnie. The zoo had
    many different animals.
    It had 12 deer and 26 monkeys.
    It also had 38 birds. How many
    animals and birds is this in all?

    There were _____ animals
    and birds in all.

11. 100 + 20 + 500 + 60 =

    Answer: _____

12. 92 + 8 + 64 + 36 =

    Answer: _____

13. 30 + 22 + 30 + 44 =

    Answer: _____

14. 25 + 25 + 50 + 75 =

    Answer: _____

(Answers on page 163)

ADDING AND SUBTRACTING WITHIN 1000

2.NBT.B.7 Add and subtract within 1000, using concrete models or drawings and strategies based on place value, properties of operations, and/or the relationship between addition and subtraction; relate the strategy to a written method. Understand that in adding or subtracting thee-digit numbers, one adds or subtracts hundreds and hundreds, tens and tens, ones and ones; and sometimes it is necessary to compose or decompose tens or hundreds.

Answer these subtraction and addition problems where **Each bar = 100** .

1.

—

Ⓐ 20   Ⓒ 300
Ⓑ 200   Ⓓ 600

2.

+

Ⓐ 70   Ⓒ 700
Ⓑ 300   Ⓓ 90

3. Nicholas collects shells that he finds on the beach. He has 600 small white shells and 300 black shells. How many shells does he have?

Ⓐ 800   Ⓒ 600
Ⓑ 900   Ⓓ 200

+

Number and Operations in Base Ten

112

4. Which shows 402 + 200?

☐ = 100   ◯ = 1

Ⓐ ☐☐☐☐☐☐◯◯

Ⓑ ☐☐☐☐◯◯◯◯

Ⓒ ☐☐☐☐◯◯◯◯◯

Ⓓ ☐☐◯◯◯◯◯◯

5. 800 + 50 = 400 + 400 + ☐
- Ⓐ 30 + 30
- Ⓑ 20 + 30
- Ⓒ 40 − 10
- Ⓓ 40 + 20

6. 800 = 1000 − ☐
- Ⓐ 300
- Ⓑ 200
- Ⓒ 400
- Ⓓ 600

7. 1000 − 90 = 900 + 10

  True   False

8. 250 + 250 = 1000 − 500

  True   False

9.   5 6 0
       − 1 3 8
       ‾‾‾‾‾‾‾

- Ⓐ 422
- Ⓑ 622
- Ⓒ 438
- Ⓓ 430

10.   7 0 5
        − 1 3 2
        ‾‾‾‾‾‾‾

- Ⓐ 633
- Ⓑ 673
- Ⓒ 573
- Ⓓ 533

(Answers on page 164–165)

MEASURING

2.MD.A.1 Measure the length of an object by selecting and using appropriate tools such as rulers, yardsticks, meter sticks, and measuring tapes.

2.MD.A.2 Measure the length of an object twice, using length units of different lengths for the two measurements; describe how the two measurements relate to the size of the unit chosen.

1. What would be best to use to measure the length of your foot?
   - Ⓐ a ruler
   - Ⓑ a yardstick
   - Ⓒ a meter stick
   - Ⓓ a scale

2. What would be the best tool to use to measure the length of the classroom?
   - Ⓐ a ruler
   - Ⓑ a yardstick
   - Ⓒ a meter stick
   - Ⓓ measuring tape

3. About how long is this rectangle?

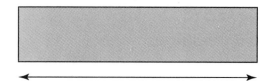

   - Ⓐ 2 feet long
   - Ⓑ 2 centimeters long
   - Ⓒ 2 inches long
   - Ⓓ 2 yards long

4. Jacob's dad is very tall. Which measurement below could be his dad's height?
   - Ⓐ 3 feet tall
   - Ⓑ 6 feet tall
   - Ⓒ 12 inches tall
   - Ⓓ 1 yard tall

5. About how long is a real car?
   - Ⓐ 18 feet long
   - Ⓑ 18 centimeters long
   - Ⓒ 18 inches long
   - Ⓓ 18 miles long

6. Circle the BIGGEST unit.

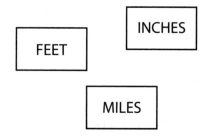

7. Use the *inch* ruler in the picture to measure.

How tall is the bottle of water below?

The bottle is about _____ inches tall.

If Danny filled the bottle only half full,
how many inches tall would that be?

Half the bottle would be

_____ inches tall.

Billy filled the bottle to the top.
Then, he shared the water with
4 people. How many inches
of water would each person get?

Each person would get _____ inches
of water from this bottle.

8. We measured the top of the teacher's desk.

Carlito said it measured 4 feet long.

Allyssa said it measured 48 inches long.

Could they both be correct?

Yes   No

How do you know?

_____

_____

_____

_____

(Answers on page 165)

MEASURING AND COMPARING

2.MD.A.3 Estimate lengths using units of inches, feet, centimeters, and meters.

2.MD.A.4 Measure to determine how much longer one object is than another, expressing the length differences in terms of a standard length unit.

1. About how long is your shortest finger?
   - (A) 3–4 inches
   - (B) 3–4 cm
   - (C) 1 foot
   - (D) 1 meter

2. About how wide is this piece of paper?
   - (A) 8 inches
   - (B) 2 inches
   - (C) 2 feet
   - (D) 1 yard

5. If you were to **add** the lengths of these 3 paper clips together, they would be about _____ long.
   - (A) 1 yard
   - (B) 1 foot
   - (C) 9 centimeters
   - (D) 3 centimeters

3. About how long is a new pencil?
   - (A) one yard
   - (B) one foot
   - (C) 6 inches
   - (D) 2 meters

6. If you were to measure the width of 3 **real** apples, they would measure about ?
   - (A) **24 cm** = 8 cm + 8 cm + 8 cm
   - (B) **30 in.** = 10 in. + 10 in. + 10 in.
   - (C) **3 feet** = 1 ft. + 1 ft. + 1 ft.
   - (D) **2 meters** = 1 m + 1 m

4. Which is the longest measurement?
   - (A) 10 centimeters
   - (B) 10 inches
   - (C) 10 yards
   - (D) 10 meters

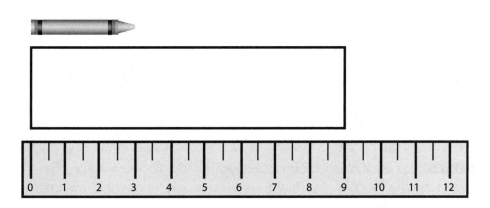

7. Use the picture of the small crayon, white paper, and ruler shown above. About how long is the crayon?

The crayon is about _____ inches long.

8. Here is a picture of a father and his young daughter. The father is 6 feet tall and his daughter is 3 feet tall. How do their heights compare?
Who is taller?

_____

9. Ann wants to make copies of this picture of a kitten.

She wants to paste them one next to the other from the left to the right side of this paper.

About how many of these pictures does she need?

Fill in your answer circle below.

<4   5   6   >6

○   ○   ○   ○

(Answers on pages 165–166)

ADDING AND SUBTRACTING LENGTHS WITH NANCY

> **2.MD.B.5** Use addition and subtraction within 100 to solve word problems involving lengths that are given in the same units, e.g., by using drawings (e.g., rulers) and equations with a symbol for the unknown number to represent the problem.

1. Nancy had a long strip of paper that was 18 inches long. She cut off 10 inches to write on. How long was the strip of paper that was left?

2. Nancy's grandmother had a long roll of ribbon. It was 12 feet long. She used 6 feet to wrap gifts.

   How many feet are left? _____

3. The kitchen table measures 5 feet long.

   How long would 3 tables be all together? _____

4. Nancy's mom bought a rug for the hall. It measured 36 inches + another 36 inches long. How many **inches** long is the rug in all?

36 inches long	36 inches long

   Answer: _____ inches long in all.

5. The driveway at Nancy's house is 40 feet long. Her mother's car is 18 feet long. Her dad's car is 19 feet long. Do both cars fit in the driveway? (Circle your answer below.)

Yes   No   How do you know? _____

6. The number lines below show three lengths of rope that Nancy found. What are the three lengths?

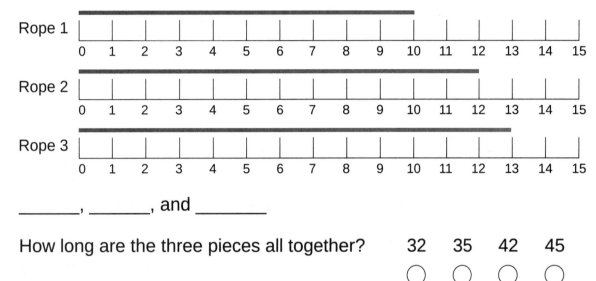

Rope 1
0 1 2 3 4 5 6 7 8 9 10 11 12 13 14 15

Rope 2
0 1 2 3 4 5 6 7 8 9 10 11 12 13 14 15

Rope 3
0 1 2 3 4 5 6 7 8 9 10 11 12 13 14 15

_____, _____, and _____

How long are the three pieces all together?   32   35   42   45
                                                  ○   ○   ○   ○

7. Nancy's dad is making a picture frame. He cut 2 pieces of wood. Each piece was 18 inches long. He cut 2 more pieces of wood. Each piece was 12 inches long. How many inches of wood did he cut in all?

     50   52   58   60
      ○   ○   ○   ○

8. On Saturday, Nancy and her dad used a tape measure to measure the living room. It measured 18 feet long and 13 feet wide. Why did they use a tape measure instead of a 12-inch ruler?

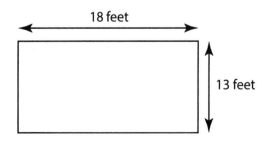

_____

(Answers on page 166)

NUMBERS, MEASURING, AND NUMBER LINES

2.MD.B.6 Represent whole numbers as lengths from 0 on a number-line diagram with equally spaced points corresponding to the numbers 0, 1, 2, and represent whole-number sums and differences within 100 on a number-line diagram.

1. **Write** the numbers 3–10 to complete the number line below.

0   1   2

Draw a line under the number line that is 6 units long.

2. **Write** the numbers 1–9 to complete the number line below.

0   10

Show how you would represent 3 + 6 on the number line.

What is the sum of 3 + 6? _____

3. **Write** the numbers 1–9 to complete the number line below.

0   10

Show how you would represent 8 – 2 on the number line above.

What is the difference between 8 and 2? _____

If Trey had 8 markers and gave 2 markers to his sister, how many markers would he have left?

He would have _____ markers left.

4. **Write** the numbers 71–79 to complete the number line below.

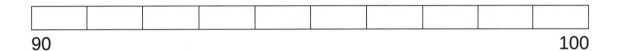

70   80

Show how you would represent 78 – 3 on the number line.

What is the difference between 78 and 3? _____

Does this match what you drew on your number line?

Yes __ No __

5. Use the number line below to teach a first grade student how to add 92 and 5 more.

90   100

What is the sum of 92 and 5 more? _____

6.
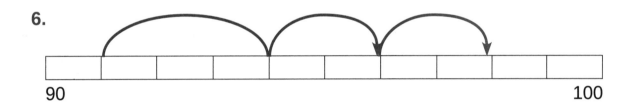

90   100

Write a number sentence that matches what this number line shows.

_____ ( ) _____ ( ) _____ ( ) _____ ( ) _____

7.

40	42	44	46	48	50	52	54	56	58	60

My father went shopping for grandpa's birthday gift.
He had $58 and spent $42 on a shirt for grandpa.

Use the number line above to help you.

How much money did my father have left? _____

Did he have enough money to buy my mother a scarf for $15?

Yes _____ No _____

Explain how you know.

_____

_____

_____

_____

8.

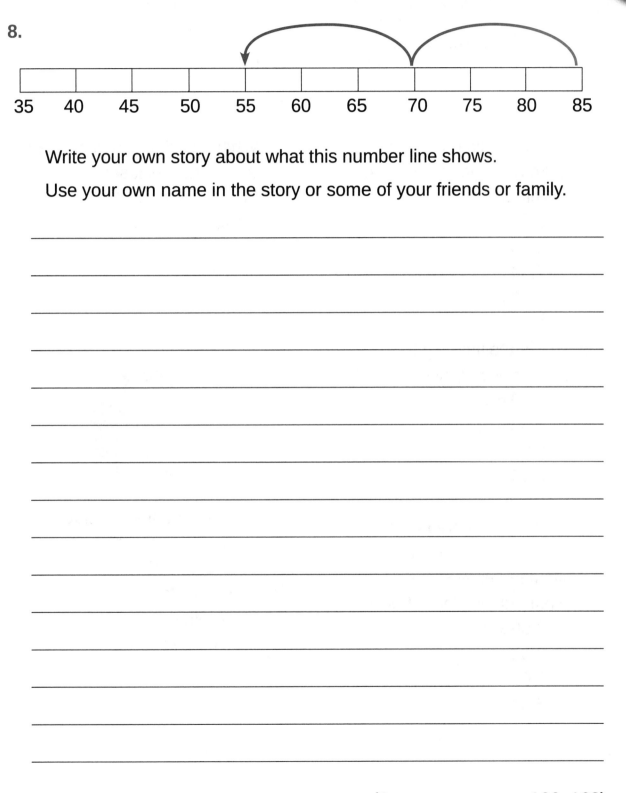

Write your own story about what this number line shows.

Use your own name in the story or some of your friends or family.

_____

_____

_____

_____

_____

_____

_____

_____

_____

_____

_____

_____

_____

(Answers on pages 166–168)

WORKING WITH TIME AND MONEY

2.MD.C.7 Tell and write time from analog and digital clocks to the nearest five minutes, using A.M. and P.M.

2.MD.C.8 Solve word problems involving dollar bills, quarters, dimes, nickels, and pennies, using $ and cent symbols appropriately.

1. This is the time many children wake up to go to school in the morning.
   Ⓐ 2:00 P.M.
   Ⓑ 6:00 P.M.
   Ⓒ 7:00 A.M.
   Ⓓ 2:00 A.M.

2. This is the time my 6-year-old brother usually goes to bed.
   Ⓐ 2:00 P.M.
   Ⓑ 5:00 P.M.
   Ⓒ 8:00 P.M.
   Ⓓ 2:30 A.M.

3. When I ate **breakfast** this morning, the digital clock said five minutes after seven.
   What did the clock show?
   Ⓐ 7:05 A.M.
   Ⓑ 7:05 P.M.
   Ⓒ 5:07 A.M.
   Ⓓ 5:07 P.M.

4. When I had **lunch** yesterday, the digital clock said ten minutes after twelve.
   What did the clock show?
   Ⓐ 12:10 A.M.
   Ⓑ 12:10 P.M.
   Ⓒ 10:12 P.M.
   Ⓓ 10:12 A.M.

5. What time does the clock above show?
   Ⓐ two o'clock
   Ⓑ one o'clock
   Ⓒ two-thirty
   Ⓓ ten minutes after twelve

6. Put these times in order. Write on the lines below.
Begin with the earliest morning time.

11:00 A.M.   3:30 P.M.   8:15 A.M.   12 Noon   9:30 P.M.

_____   _____   _____   _____   _____

7. Robbie ate breakfast at
7:00 A.M., and he ate lunch
at 12 Noon. How many hours
were there between his
breakfast and lunch?

There were _____ hours
between his breakfast and
lunch.

8. Which time matches the clock
above?
Ⓐ 6:30
Ⓑ 5:30
Ⓒ 5:25
Ⓓ 6:25

9. Jamal says the clock below
shows five minutes after three
o'clock. Henrique says it
shows fifteen minutes after
one o'clock.

Who is correct?

_____

How do you know?

_____

_____

125

10. If you have 3 dimes and 2 pennies, how many cents do you have?

Ⓐ 3¢

Ⓑ 32¢

Ⓒ 23¢

Ⓓ 230¢

11. If you have 2 quarters and 3 dimes, how many cents do you have?

Ⓐ 53 cents

Ⓑ 70 cents

Ⓒ 80 cents

Ⓓ 203 cents

12. Kaitlyn has 8 dollars and 2 quarters. How much money does she have?

Ⓐ $8.25

Ⓑ $8.050

Ⓒ $85.00

Ⓓ $8.50

13. Her brother Tyler has 6 dollars, 3 dimes, and 1 nickel. How much money does he have?

Ⓐ $6.53

Ⓑ $6.35

Ⓒ $63.50

Ⓓ $635

14. Tim has 1 quarter, 2 dimes, and 8 pennies.

Glenn has 2 quarters, and 5 dimes.

Who has the most money?

_____ has the most money.

How much more money does he have?

He has _____ more.

15. Glenn emptied his toy bank and found the coins shown below.

Which coins should he use first if he wants to add to see how much money he has?

He should use the _____ first. Why?

_____

_____

How much money does he have in all?

He has _____ cents in all.

Does he have enough money to buy candy for 35 cents and a small toy for 40 cents?

Yes _____ No _____

Explain in words, or draw a picture or diagram, to explain your answer above.

```



```

(Answers on pages 168–169)

LINE PLOTS, CHARTS, AND TALLY MARKS

> **2.MD.D.9** Generate measurement data by measuring lengths of several objects to the nearest whole unit, or by making repeated measurements of the same object. Show the measurements by making a line plot, where the horizontal scale is marked off in whole-number units.

1. Circle the group that has more.

2. Circle the 2 groups with the same number of objects.

3.

Pet	Tally
Cat	卌 卌 II
Fish	卌 IIII
Dog	卌 IIII
Turtle	卌 III

Which pet has 12 tally marks?

_____ has 12 tally marks.

Which two animals have the same number of tally marks?

_____ and _____

4. This table shows the fruit students said they like best.

Fruit	Tally
watermelon	卌 卌 II
banana	卌 IIII
peach	卌 卌
apple	卌 III
grapes	卌 卌 III

Which fruit was chosen most often?

_____

Which fruit was chosen the fewest times?

_____

5. Louis asked all the boys and girls in his class what color balloons they liked best. Louis picked yellow for himself. See his chart below.

Color	Balloons								
red									
blue									
yellow									

0   1   2   3   4   5   6   7   8   9

Which color balloon was chosen most often? _____

How many boys and girls said *blue* was their favorite? _____

How many boys and girls are in Louis' class? _____

More than half the boys and girls chose yellow. Yes_____ No _____

6. Johnnie and his sister live in California. They made a graph of some of their favorite toys.

Balls	soccer	beach	baseball	football
Cards	animals	pets	letters	numbers
Drawing	pencils	crayons	paint	chalk
Puzzles	farm	city	zoo	

Which kind of toys are best used outside? _____

Name 2 toys used for drawing. _____ and _____

How many different types of puzzles do they have? _____

7. The line plot below shows how many second grade students
   ate fruit with breakfast last week. Each X = 5 students.

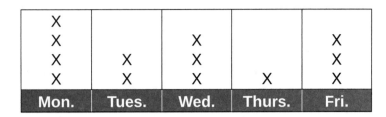

How many students ate fruit on Wednesday? _____

Which day had the fewest number of students who ate fruit for
breakfast that day? _____

How many students had fruit that morning? _____

How many students ate fruit for breakfast on Monday **and** Tuesday
together? _____

There were 95 second graders in school on Tuesday. How many
did NOT eat fruit for breakfast that day? _____

8. Mrs. Blake's second grade class is saving money to buy pencils for
   their school fundraiser. The line plot below shows what they have
   saved so far. Each X = 10 students.

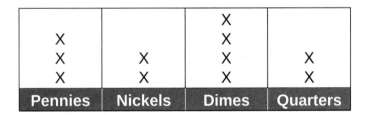

How many *nickels* did they save? They saved _____ nickels.

How much money did they save in *pennies?* _____ cents.

Do they have more *pennies* or more *quarters*? More _____

(Answers on pages 169–170)

SHAPES

2.G.A.1 Recognize and draw shapes having specified attributes, such as a given number of angles or a given number of equal faces. Identify triangles, quadrilaterals, pentagons, hexagons, and cubes.

1. What 2-dimensional shape has exactly 4 sides?
   Ⓐ a triangle
   Ⓑ a pentagon
   Ⓒ a hexagon
   Ⓓ a quadrilateral

2. Name a flat shape that has only 3 sides.
   Ⓐ triangle
   Ⓑ pentagon
   Ⓒ hexagon
   Ⓓ quadrilateral

3. Which shapes have **more than** four angles and four sides?

   Circle all of your answers.

   triangle   kite   pentagon

   hexagon   rectangle   square

4. Which shape has exactly five angles and five sides?
   Ⓐ a triangle
   Ⓑ a pentagon
   Ⓒ a hexagon
   Ⓓ a rectangle

5. What is the name of this shape?

   Ⓐ a triangle
   Ⓑ a rectangle
   Ⓒ a pentagon
   Ⓓ a hexagon

6. How many angles does a hexagon have?
   Ⓐ 3
   Ⓑ 4
   Ⓒ 5
   Ⓓ 6

7. Circle the picture of a *cube*.

   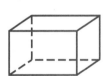

8. Circle the pictures of a *cone.*

9. A box is often shaped like a *cube.*   Yes _____   No _____

The top of a desk looks like a *rectangle.*   Yes _____   No _____

An apple is shaped like a *cone.*   Yes _____   No _____

Most television screens are shaped like a *circle.*   Yes _____   No _____

A ring is a *circle* shape.   Yes _____   No _____

10. **Draw** a *triangle* on top of the *rectangle* below.

11. **Draw** a big *rectangle*, then draw a *circle* inside the rectangle.

12. Circle the shapes below that have *equal faces*.

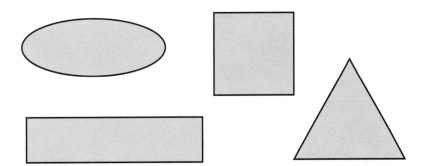

13. Nicholas and Samantha are comparing shapes. Samantha says a square is also a quadrilateral.

    Is she correct? Yes _____ No ___

(Answers on page 171)

RECTANGLES AND CIRCLES

> **2.G.A.2** Partition a rectangle into rows and columns of same-size squares and count to find the total number of them.
>
> **2.G.A.3** Partition circles and rectangles into two, three, or four equal shares, describe the shares using the words halves, thirds, half of, a third of, etc., and describe the whole as two halves, three thirds, four fourths. Recognize that equal shares of identical wholes need not have the same shape.

1. What is the total number of small squares in this shape?

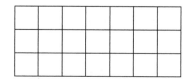

- Ⓐ 12
- Ⓑ 15
- Ⓒ 21
- Ⓓ 24

2. What is the total number of shaded squares in this shape?

- Ⓐ 6
- Ⓑ 8
- Ⓒ 12
- Ⓓ 24

3. This whole circle =
- Ⓐ three thirds
- Ⓑ four fourths
- Ⓒ four halves
- Ⓓ five fifths

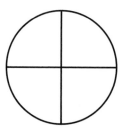

4. What part of this circle is shaded?

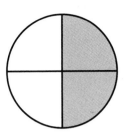

Ⓐ one third
Ⓑ one half
Ⓒ one fourth
Ⓓ one fifth

5. Each part of this circle =

Ⓐ $\frac{1}{2}$

Ⓑ $\frac{1}{3}$

Ⓒ $\frac{1}{4}$

Ⓓ $\frac{1}{5}$

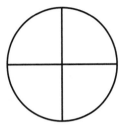

6. Jasmine ate half of a cupcake. What part of the cupcake is left?

Ⓐ one half
Ⓑ one third
Ⓒ one fourth
Ⓓ one fifth

7. This rectangle is divided into

Ⓐ thirds
Ⓑ fourths
Ⓒ fifths
Ⓓ sixths

8. Jordie's mother cut one fourth of the sheet cake to save for tomorrow. How much of the cake is left?

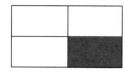

_____ of the cake is left.

9. One 20-inch pizza pie is cut into fourths. Another 20-inch pizza pie is cut into sixths. Which pizza pie has the **larger slices**?
Ⓐ the one cut into fourths
Ⓑ the one cut into sixths
Ⓒ they are all the same size

10. The busy freeway is divided into 5 lanes. One lane is an express lane. What part of the freeway is **not** used as an express lane?

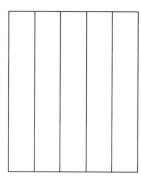

Ⓐ one fifth
Ⓑ two fifths
Ⓒ three fifths
Ⓓ four fifths

11. Abigayle is planting a garden with her mother. She planted corn in *one third* of the garden. Her mother planted tomatoes in another *third* of the garden. How much of the garden is left for other vegetables?
Ⓐ one fourth
Ⓑ two fourths
Ⓒ one third
Ⓓ two thirds

12. Matilda helped her grandpa bake cookies. She added *half* a bag of chips to the cookie mix. How much of the chips were left for next time?
Ⓐ one third of the bag
Ⓑ one half of the bag
Ⓒ one fourth of the bag
Ⓓ one fifth of the bag

(Answers on page 172)

MATH
PRACTICE TEST

1. Count by fives and fill in the missing numbers.

   315, _____ 325, _____ 335, 340

NOTE

A 12 inch ruler is needed.

2. Count by fives and fill in the missing numbers.

   175, _____ 185, _____ 195, 200

3. Johnnie and his dad drove 3 hours to Nevada.
   Then they drove 4 more hours to Los Angeles and 2 more
   hours to San Diego.

   How many hours did they drive in all?

   They drove _____ hours in all.

4. Samantha and her dad drove 90 miles to New Jersey, then 45 miles
   to New York, and 200 miles more to Virginia.

   How many miles did they drive in all?

   They drove _____ miles in all.

5. What is true about the number **562**?

   A. It is > 559.   Yes _____   No _____

   B. It has 5 ones.   Yes _____   No _____

   C. It is an odd number.   Yes _____   No _____

   D. It is between 560 and 565.   Yes _____   No _____

   E. It has six hundreds.   Yes _____   No _____

   F. 562 + 8 = 570.   Yes _____   No _____

6. What is true about **427**?

   A. It is < 431.   Yes _____   No _____

   B. It has 2 tens.   Yes _____   No _____

   C. It is an even number.   Yes _____   No _____

   D. It is between 425 and 430.   Yes _____   No _____

   E. It has seven hundreds.   Yes _____   No _____

   F. 200 + 200 + 27 = 427.   Yes _____   No _____

7. There were 40 goldfish in the big fish tank in the pet store. Eliza's dad bought 3 of them to bring home.

   How many goldfish were left in the big fish tank?

   There were _____ goldfish left in the big fish tank.

8. There were 20 angel fish in the smaller fish tank at the pet store. Johnnie's mom bought 3 of them to bring home and 3 more to give to a friend.

   How many angel fish were left in the smaller fish tank?

   There were _____ angel fish left in the smaller fish tank.

9. Johnnie and his mom left home at 11:00 A.M. to go to the pet store. They came home at 15 minutes after one o'clock.

   Circle the time they came home.

       12:45 P.M.   1:00 P.M.   1:15 P.M.   1:05 P.M.

10. Eliza and her dad left home at 1:00 P.M. to go to the pet store. They came home 30 minutes after 2 o'clock.

    Circle the time they came home.

        2:00 P.M.   2:30 P.M.   2:45 P.M.   2:15 P.M.

11. On Saturday, Eliza and her dad bought food for a family picnic. They bought 12 hamburgers and 16 hot dogs. They also bought 12 round-rolls, 16 long-rolls, and 1 large watermelon.

How many round-rolls and long-rolls did they buy all together?

They bought _____ rolls all together.

Eliza ate 1 hot dog and her dad ate 2 hot dogs. How many hot dogs were left?

_____ hot dogs were left.

Write the number sentence in the box below to show how many hot dogs were left.

```
┌─────────────────────────────────────────────┐
│                                               │
│                                               │
│                                               │
│                                               │
└─────────────────────────────────────────────┘
```

12. On Tuesday, Johnnie and his mom went to the farmers' market in the big city. They bought fruit for their trip. They bought 5 apples, 8 oranges, 5 pears, and 2 bananas.

How many pieces of fruit did they buy all together?

They bought _____ pieces of fruit all together.

Johnnie gave 3 pieces of fruit to his friends. How many pieces of fruit were left?

There were _____ pieces of fruit left.

13. Dan and his older son washed the windows in their house.
The first floor has 12 big windows and 2 small windows.
The first floor also has a garage with 3 more windows.
The second floor has 8 big windows and 2 small windows.

How many windows are there in all?

There are _____ windows in all.

How many more windows are on the first floor than on the second floor?

There are _____ more windows on the first floor.

14. Eliza's mom works in a big office building in the city. She counted 22 windows on the first floor. Then she counted 30 windows on the second floor and 30 windows on the third floor.

How many windows did she count in all?

She counted _____ windows in all.

How many more windows are on the third floor than on the first floor?

There are _____ more windows on the third floor than on the first floor.

15. The seats in the school auditorium are numbered.
If the pattern below continues, what are the missing seat numbers?

Seat 133, 135, _____, _____, _____, 143, 145, 147, _____

16. The grade 2 classes sat in the first rows in the auditorium. They used **82** seats. The grade 3 classes sat behind them and used **96** seats.

How many seats did they use all together?

They used _____ seats all together.

17. In Eliza's new school there are **45** students in kindergarten, **55** students in grade 1, **50** students in grade 2, and **60** students in grade 3.

How many students are in the new school?

_____ students are in the new school.

How many more students are in grade 3 than in kindergarten?

_____ more students.

18. The library in the new school has many new books. So far, they have counted 200 animal books, 300 science books, and 250 story books.

How many books did they count so far?

_____ books.

If the school buys 125 more books, how many books will they have then?

_____ books.

In the box below, explain how you know.

Use the table below to answer questions 19–21.

Item	Cost
Brian	3 dimes and 2 pennies
Venice	2 quarters
Marissa	1 quarter and 1 nickel
Jeff	2 quarters and 4 nickels
Jodi	6 dimes and 10 pennies
Devon	3 quarters and 2 pennies

19. Which two people have the same amount of money?

_____ and _____.

20. How much money do they *each* have?

They each have _____ cents.

21. Who has the most money?

_____ has the most money.

Use the Dollar Store prices on the chart to answer questions 22–24.

The Dollar Store		
Balloon	75 cents	
Ball	50 cents	
Candy	90 cents	
Cookie	80 cents	
Pencil	70 cents	
Toy	90 cents	

22. Check off two items you might buy on the chart above.

23. What would be the total cost of those two items?

    _____ dollars and _____ cents.

24. How much money would it cost to buy a ball, a pencil, and a toy?

    Answer: _____.

25. What is the difference between 582 and 342?

    Answer: _____.

26. What is the difference between 53 and 23?

    Answer: _____.

27. Circle the **smallest** sum.

        146 + 36   150 + 28   35 + 145

28. Circle the **largest** sum.

        123 + 48   32 + 129   134 + 27

29. Johnnie was playing a card game with his brother.
They had 26 red cards and 26 black cards.

How many cards did they have in all?

They had _____ cards in all.

If 12 cards had pictures on them and the others did not, how many cards did NOT have pictures on them?

_____ cards did NOT have pictures on them.

Explain how you know in the box below.

30. Eliza's cousin had many beads in a big box. She had 20 red beads, 35 white beads, 25 blue beads, and 12 pink beads.

   How many beads did she have in all?

   She had _____ beads in all.

   How many more white beads did she have than pink beads?

   She had _____ more white beads than pink beads.

31. I have only 3 sides and 3 angles. What am I?

   Circle your answer.

   a rectangle   a square   a kite   a triangle

32. I have 4 sides and 4 angles. All my sides are the same length.

   What am I? Circle your answer.

   a circle   a cone   a triangle   a square   a pentagon

33. Use a ruler and measure the line drawn below.

   ●━━━━━━━━━━━━━━━━━━━━━━━━━━━●

   This line measures about _____ inches long.

34. Use a ruler to measure how tall this workbook is.

   Circle your answer. This workbook page is about

   5 inches tall   **8** inches tall   **11** inches tall   **14** inches tall

35. Circle the picture of a cube below.

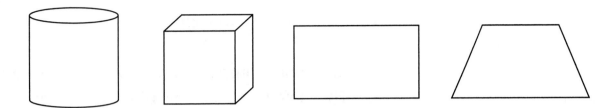

36. What part of the circle is shaded?

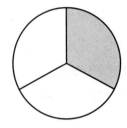

   Ⓐ   one fifth

   Ⓑ   one fourth

   Ⓒ   one third

   Ⓓ   one half

37. Jacob ate half of a candy bar. What part of the candy bar is left?

   Ⓐ   one third

   Ⓑ   one fourth

   Ⓒ   one half

   Ⓓ   one fifth

38. Shade in one fourth of the large rectangle below.

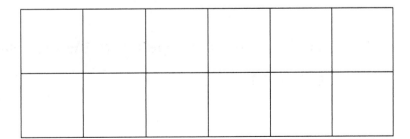

Read the story below and then answer questions 39–42.

Juan and Marissa Go Shopping

Juan and his baby sister, Marissa, spent time on Saturday shopping with their mother and grandmother. They left their house at 10 o'clock in the morning. They drove to a shoe store and spent $25 on a pair of shoes for Juan. They also bought 4 pairs of socks for Marissa. The 4 pairs of socks cost 8 dollars in all. Grandma bought shoe polish that cost 2 dollars and a pair of slippers that cost 20 dollars.

Next, they stopped at the drug store for grandma's pills. Grandma bought 1 bottle of pills and 4 bottles of vitamins. All together she spent $20. Juan's mother bought some cards and spent $6. She surprised Juan and Marissa and bought them one set of bubbles. The bubbles cost 3 dollars.

39. How much did Marissa's 4 pairs of socks cost?

The 4 pairs of socks cost _____.

40. How much does 1 pair of socks cost?

One pair of socks cost _____.

41. How much more did Juan's shoes cost than Marissa's 4 pairs of socks?
Juan's shoes cost 25 dollars. Marissa's socks cost 8 dollars.

Juan's shoes cost _____ dollars more than Marissa's socks.

42. How much money did they spend all together at the drug store?
Write the number sentence for this total.

_____ (+) _____ (+) _____ = _____

All together they spent _____ dollars at the drug store.

Read the story below and then answer questions 43–50.

A New Pet

Nancy, her sister Marie, and their mom drove 5 miles to the new pet store. They saw little puppies, some kittens, and a big fish tank. Nancy counted 22 little gray fish, 10 goldfish, and 12 angelfish. Marie saw a big black dog with 8 little puppies. She also saw a poodle with 5 puppies. Their mom said they came here to buy a new puppy. They picked a cute black-and-white puppy. The pet store owner told Nancy and Marie that the puppy is 10 weeks old and weighs 8 pounds. The puppy costs $80 and the puppy collar costs $15.

Next, they drove to the food store. They bought puppy food and a box of cookie bones. The dog food cost 50 cents for one can, and 2 dollars for one box of cookie bones. They bought **5 cans** of dog food and **1 box** of cookie bones. The new puppy was very tired. He slept for 3 hours when they came home. When he woke up, he jumped and played and ate some dog food. Nancy and Marie named him Happy. Happy stays in the kitchen during the night. He sleeps in a little box with a warm blanket.

43. How many fish did Nancy count?

    Write the number sentence for this.

    _____ (   ) _____ (   ) _____ = _____

44. Which dog had the most puppies?

    _____

45. How many more puppies did that dog have than the other dog?

    She had _____ more puppies.

46. How much money did the puppy and the puppy's collar cost?

    _____ (+) _____ = _____ dollars.

47. How much money did they spend at the food store for puppy food and cookie bones? (Show your work.)

All together they spent _____ dollars on puppy food and cookie bones.

48. The puppy fell asleep at 2:00. What time did he wake up?

Circle your answer.

    3:00   4:00   4:30   5:00   6:00

49. Happy weighed only 8 pounds when he came to live with Nancy and her family. He will gain about 25 pounds each year for the next 2 years. About how many pounds will Happy weigh when he is 2 years old?

_____ (____) _____ (____) _____ = _____ pounds

50. What weighs about the same as Happy now? Circle your answer.
- Ⓐ one apple
- Ⓑ one pencil
- Ⓒ a large bag of apples
- Ⓓ a small cookie

(Answers on pages 173–176)

MATH ANSWERS EXPLAINED

OPERATIONS AND ALGEBRAIC THINKING

Adding and Subtracting within 100
(2.OA.A.1), pages 88–89

1. **(C) $61**   Decompose 25: $25 = 20 + 5$

    $25 + 40 - 4 =$ $20 + 5 + 40 - 4$

    Put the 10's and one's together $20 + 40 + 5 - 4$

    $60 \quad + \quad 1$

    61

2. **(D) 20** $65 - 5 + ? = 80$ $65 - 5 = 60$ $60 + 20 = 80$

3. **80**   6 sets of 10s = 60

    2 sets of 10s = 20

    8 sets of 10s = 80

4. **$10**   Tara and Zak have $20 + $30 = $50 together.

    $60 - 50 = $10 more that they need

5. **13**

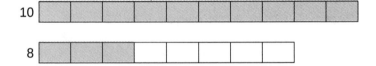

Tens	Ones
1	8
−	5
1	**3**

or

6. **27 crayons are in the smaller box.**

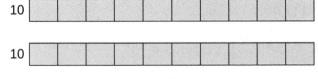

Tens	Ones	
3	9	
− 1	2	
2	**7**	

or

39 − 12 = **27**

155

7.   35 (+) 20 (−) 5 (=) = 50

8.

A.	The sum is larger than 80.	No	55 + 23 = 78
			78 is not larger than 80
B.	The sum is smaller than 75.	No	78 > 75
C.	The sum is 78.	Yes	
D.	The sum is less than 90 − 5.	Yes	90 − 5 = 85
			78 is less than 85.

Practice to Become Fluent: Add and Subtract within 100, pages 90–91

1.	18	14.	40	27.	40	40.	14
2.	50	15.	6	28.	40	41.	40
3.	88	16.	90	29.	30	42.	10
4.	58	17.	6	30.	25	43.	20
5.	28	18.	60	31.	25	44.	24
6.	100	19.	20	32.	10	45.	60
7.	66	20.	5	33.	10	46.	35
8.	97	21.	2	34.	22	47.	100
9.	22	22.	6	35.	42	48.	6
10.	100	23.	5	36.	16	49.	60
11.	92	24.	10	37.	60	50.	20
12.	32	25.	5	38.	22		
13.	4	26.	60	39.	83		

Adding and Subtracting Fluently (2.OA.B.2), pages 92–93

1.	(C) 19, 10 + 9 = 19	8.	6	15.	8
2.	(B) 13, 6 + 7 = 13	9.	12	16.	18
3.	(B) 17, 7 + 10 = 17	10.	18	17.	18
4.	(B) 8, 12 − 4 = 8	11.	14	18.	14
5.	(B) 18, 8 + 10 = 18	12.	11	19.	17
6.	(D) 13, 16 − 3 = 13	13.	14	20.	19
7.	16	14.	14		

Even and Odd Numbers (2.OA.C.3), pages 94–95

1.   (A)   even   Notice when you count by 2s there are none left over.

2.   (B)   odd   There are 11 ◎s here. If you divide this into 2 groups you would have 1 ◎ left over.

3.   (B)   odd   9 things cannot be made into 2 even groups.

4.   (B)   odd   9 − 4 = 5   Notice that an odd number minus an even number is an odd number. Possible drawings can look like this:

5.   (A)   even   14 + 4 + 2 = 18 + 2 = 20   Any number that has zero in the ones place can be divided into 2 even groups.
10 = 5 + 5 or 30 = 15 + 15

6.   4 + 4 = 8

7.   A.   Yes   15 is odd.   7 + 7 + 1 = 15
     B.   No   20 is not odd; 20 is even.   10 + 10 = 20
     C.   No   13 is not even; 13 is odd.   6 + 6 + 1 = 13
     D.   No   6 is not odd; 6 is even.   3 + 3 = 6
     E.   Yes   5 is odd   2 + 2 + 1 = 5

8.   A.   Even   14 is an even number.   7 + 7 = 14
     B.   Odd   19 is an odd number.   9 + 9 + 1 = 19
     C.   Odd   9 is an odd number.   4 + 4 + 1 = 9
     D.   Even   16 is an even number.   8 + 8 = 16
     E.   Odd   11 is an odd number.   5 + 5 + 1 = 11

9.   Answers could be 12, 14, 16, or 18.

10. A.   Even   A donkey has 4 feet.
                 2 + 2 = 4; 4 is an even number

11. A.   Even   15 + 3 = 18   18 is an even number.
     B.   Even   4 + 4 = 8
     C.   Even   8 + 8 = 16
     D.   Odd   7 + 8 = 15   7 + 7 + 1 = 15   15 is an odd number.
     E.   Odd   6 + 1 = 7   3 + 3 + 1 = 7   7 is an odd number.

12. 5 and 17 are odd numbers.   5 = 2 + 2 + 1   17 = 8 + 8 + 1

13. odd   3 + 2 + 1 = 6   5 + 4 + 6 = 15   6 + 15 = 21   21 is an odd number

Using Rows and Columns (2.OA.C.4), pages 96–97

1.   **(C)**   3 + 3 + 3 = 9

2.   **(B)**   4 + 4 + 4 + 4 = 16

3.   **(D)**   3 + 3 = 6

4.   **(C)**   4 + 4 = 8

5.   **5** (+) **5** (+) **5 = 15**   Count by 5s.
     3 (+) **3** (+) **3** (+) **3** (+) **3 = 15**   Count by 3s.

6.   **4 + 4 + 4 = 12**
     3 rows of **4** diamonds

7.   **6 + 6 = 12**

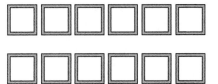

8. Answers may vary. Any 2 shaded rows of 4 is correct. 4 + 4 = 8.

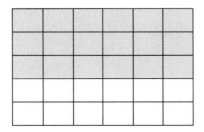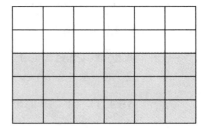

9. Answers may vary. Any 3 shaded rows of 6 is correct. 6 + 6 + 6 = 18.

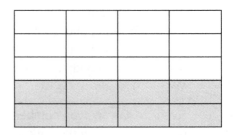

10. The following shows an array of 2 rows of 3.

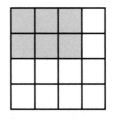

NUMBER AND OPERATIONS IN BASE TEN

Understanding 3-Digit Numbers (2.NBT.A.1), pages 98–99

1. 254   210 + 40 + 4 = 250 + 4 = 254

2. 217   100 + 100 + 10 + 7 = 200 + 10 + 7 = 217

3. A.   600 + 200 = **800**
   B.   100 + 300 = **400**
   C.   500 + 300 = **800**
   D.   400 + 500 = **900**

4.   500   5.   700
    + 100   + 200
    600   **900**

6.
```
  300
  200
+ 100
-----
  600
```

7.
```
  500
  100
+ 200
-----
  800
```

8. 200 cans of carrots
300 cans of corn
200 cans of peas
700 cans in all

9. 887 324 + 563 = 887

	Hundreds	Tens	Ones
	3	2	4
+	5	6	3
	8	8	7

10. 133 438 – 305 = 133

	Hundreds	Tens	Ones
	4	3	8
–	3	0	5
	1	3	3

11. (D) 643

12. (B) 706

13. There are (3) tens in 538.

14. There are (8) ones in 638.

15. (B) The tens place value is underlined in 824.

16. The **bolded underlined** numbers should be circled.
340 68 **7**43 **8**02 **1**99 47

17. 41, 407, 423, 429, 450

Counting by 5s, 10s, and 100s (2.NBT.A.2), pages 100–103

1. 45 and 50 Count by 5s 25, 30, 35, 40, 45, 50

2. 100 Count by 10s 60, 70, 80, 90, 100

3. (D) 80, 90 Count by 5s 70, 75, 80, 85, 90, 95, 100

4. (C) 55, 50 Count backwards by 5s 65, 60, 55, 50, 45, 40, 35
    →

    or start at 35 and count by 5s to the left
    65, 60, 55, 50, 45, 40, 35
    ←

5. (D) 500 Add 100 to each number

6. (C) 640 Add 100 to each number

7. 700 Add the 100s $200 + 500 = 700$

8. 250 Add $150 + 100$ Think: $100 + 100 = 200$, $200 + 50 = 250$

9. 650 $850 - 200 = 650$

10. 700 Subtract: $1000 - 300 = 700$
    or skip count backwards by 100s three times.
    $1000 - 100 = 900 \longrightarrow 900 - 100 = 800 \longrightarrow 800 - 100 = 700$

11. 105 cards $205 - 100 = 105$ baseball cards

12. 300 books $350 - 50 = 300$ books left on the shelves

13. 15 hits Begin at 5 and count on by 5s two more times; 5, 10, 15

14. 90 points Begin at 70 and count on by 10s two more times: 70, 80, 90

Reading and Writing Numbers to 1000 (2.NBT.A.3), pages 104–105

1. (C) two hundred fifty-six 256

2. (B) eight hundred twenty-five 825

3. (A) $520 = 500 + 20$ 5 hundreds and 2 tens

4. (D) $605 = 600 + 5$ 6 hundreds and 5 ones

5.

Hundreds	Tens	Ones
5	3	2

Answer: 3 There are **3** tens in the number 532.

6.

	Hundreds	Tens	Ones
	6	7	0
+	2	1	5
	8	8	5

Yes, the sum is 885.

7. Three hundred twelve 312
    Two hundred ninety 290
    Six hundred nineteen 619
    Two hundred six 206
    Nine hundred forty-two 942

8.   506   (five hundreds, no tens, and six ones)

9.   780   (seven hundreds, 8 tens, and no ones)

10.   none   or   0   There are no tens in the tens place in 4**0**5.

11.   six   or   6   There are 6 ones in the ones place in 59**6**.

12.   two   or   2   The number 45**2**8 has 4 thousands, 5 hundreds, **2 tens** and 8 ones.

13.   501

Comparing Two Three-Digit Numbers (2.NBT.A.4), pages 106–107

1.   <   890 < 920   890 is less than 920.
     (**8**90 has only 8 hundreds; **9**20 has 9 hundreds.)

2.   >   401 > 396   401 is greater than 396
     (**4**01 has 4 hundreds, **3**96 has only 3 hundreds.)

3.   <   468 < 472   468 is less than 472.
     (They both have 4 hundreds, so now compare the tens.
     4**6**8 has only 6 tens; 4**7**2 has 7 tens. Or you could see that 68 is less than 72, so 4**68** is less than 4**72**.)

4.   632 > 629   632 is greater than 629.
     (They both have 6 hundreds, so now compare the tens.
     6**3**2 has 3 tens; 6**2**9 has only 2 tens. Or, you could see that 32 is greater than 29, so 6**32** > 6**29**.)

5.   **6**09 is bigger than **5**09 because it has more hundreds. 609 > 509.

6.   9**1**0 is smaller than 9**5**0 because it has fewer tens. 910 < 950.

7.

10 + 2 = 12

10 + 10 = 20

20 is bigger

or use tally marks to show that 12 is smaller than 20.

8.   Use base-ten blocks or snap cubes to show that 15 < 19.

1	2	3	4	5	6	7	8	9	10	10
1	2	3	4	5	6	7	8	9		**9**

10 + 9 = 19

1	2	3	4	5	6	7	8	9	10	10
1	2	3	4	5						**5**

10 + 5 = 15

15 is smaller than 19

Use tally marks; show that 15 is smaller than 19.   H̶H̶H̶ H̶H̶H̶ H̶H̶H̶
                                                      H̶H̶H̶ H̶H̶H̶ H̶H̶H̶ IIII

9.   Ella has fewer cards.
     Miah has 28 cards; Ella has only 19 cards.
     28 has 2 tens, 19 has only 1 ten.

10. There are more buttons than paint cans.
     2**8**0 is bigger than 2**1**0.
     They both have 2 hundreds, but the buttons have 200 + **80** and the paint cans have 200 + **10**.
     8 tens is bigger than 1 ten.

11. Yes, he is correct.   600 + 200 = **800**   and   500 + 300 = **800**
     Think, the sum of 6 + 2 = **8**, and the sum of 5 + 3 = **8**.
     600 + 200 = 500 + 300

Adding and Subtracting within 100 (2.NBT.B.5), pages 108–109

			6 13					8 10
1.	65	7 3	7 3̶		2.	86	9 0	9̶ 0̶
		− 8	− 8				− 4	− 4
			6 **5**					8 6

3.   59   4.   58   5.   28   6.   27

7.   82   7 4 $\overset{1}{7}$4
            + 8   + 8̶
                    8 1̶2   Answer: 82

8.   (C)   41

9.   (D)   52

10. (A)   100   90 − 10 = 80   Think: 90 − 10 = 80   then 80 + 20 = 100

11. (D)   36   35 − 5 + 6   Think: 35 − 5 = 30   then 30 + 6 = 36

12. (C)   53   46 − 3 + 10   Think: 46 − 3 = 43   then 43 + 10 = 53

13. 50   58 − 8   Think: 50 + 8 − 8; see 50 + **8 − 8** = 50 + **0** = 50
     70   74 − 4   Think: 70 + 4 − 4 ; see 70 + **4 − 4** = 70 + **0** = 70
     4   54 − 50   Think: 50 + 4 − 50; see **50 − 50** + 4 = **0** + 4 = 4

14. 4   100 − 98 + 2   Think: 100 − 98 = 2, then 2 + 2 = 4

15. 50   40 − 20 + 30   Think: 40 − 20 = 20, then 20 + 30 = 50

16. 15   85 − 80 + 10   Think: 85 − 80 = 5, then 5 + 10 + 15

17. 23 mini cars   22 − 2 he gave to his little brother = 20 left
     Then his dad gave him 3 more, so 20 + 3 = 23.

18. 65   66 − 11 + 10   Think 66 − 11 = 55, then 55 + 10 = 65

19. 52   Think: add the three numbers of miles: 20 + 6 + 26

20. 64   50 + 20 − 6   Think: 50 + 20 = 70, then 70 − 6 = 64

21. 36   **12 + 12 + 12**   Think: **6** ones and 3 tens = 36
     69   **23 + 23 + 23**   Think: **9** ones and 6 tens = 69

22. 45   15 + 15 + 15   Think: 15 + 15 = 30, then 30 + 15 = 45

1. 41   Sometimes you can group the tens and group the **ones** to make adding easy.
          12 + **14** + **15** = 10 + 10 + 10 + **2 + 4 + 5** = 30 + **11** = 41

2. 54   Sometimes you can group numbers that add to 10, 20, 30 or 40 (a number with no ones)
          and make adding easier.
          24 + 18 + 12 = 24 + 30 = 54

3. 95   Sometimes you can group numbers that add to 50 or 100. This makes adding easier.
          30 + 45 + 20 = 20 + 30 + 45 = 50 + 45 = 95

4. 68   20 + **14** + 20 + **14** =
          40 + **14** + **14** = 40 + **28** = 68
          Sometimes you can make doubles to make adding easy.
          20 + 14 + 20 + 14 = **34** + 34 = 68

5. 69   Sometimes you can group numbers that add to 50 or 100. This makes adding easier.
          20 + **12** + 30 + **7** = 20 + 30 + **12 + 7** = 50 + **19** = 69

6. 108   **13** + **41** + **11** + **43** =   10 + 40 + 10 + 40 and **3 + 1 + 1 + 3**
                                                 50 + 50 and **4 + 4**
                                                 100 + **8**

7.   Answers will vary. They are harder to add because you need to regroup; you have more than 9
          ones (6 + 6 + 3 + 3 = 18). It also is harder because there are no zeros, and nothing adds to 50, to
          100, or to something I know just by looking at it.
          178   **56** + **66** + **33** + **23** = 50 + 60 + 30 + 20 and **6 + 6 + 3 + 3**
                                                    50 + 30 + 20 + 60 and **12 + 6**
                                                    100 + 60 and 18
                                                    160 and **18**

8. 58   16 + 24 + 18 = 40 + 18 = 58

9. 102   **64** + **38** = 90 + **12** = 102 windows

10. 76   **12** + **26** + **38** = 10 + 20 + 30 and **2 + 6 + 8**
                                     60 + **16** = 76

11. 680   100 + 500 + **20 + 60** = 600 + **80** = 680

12. 200   Sometimes you see numbers that add to 100. That makes addition easy.
          92 + 8 + 64 + 36 = 100 + 100 = 200

13. 126   30 + **22** + 30 + **44** = 30 + 30 + **22 + 44** = 60 + **66** = 126
          or
          30 + 22 + 30 + 44 = **52** + **74** =
                                     50 + 70 + **2 + 4**
                                     120 + **6** = 126

14. 175   25 + 25 + 50 + 75 = 50 + 50 + 75 = 100 + 75 = 175

1. **(B)** $400 - 200 = 200$

2. **(C)** $500 + 200 = 700$

3. **(B)**
900   600
          $+ 300$
           900   (No regrouping needed here.)

4. **(A)** $400(\square\ \square\ \square\ \square) + 200(\square\ \square) + 2(\bigcirc\ \bigcirc) = 602 = 402 + 200$

5. **(B)** $20 + 30$ $800 + 50$
              $400 + 400 + 20 + 30$

6. **(B)** 200 $800 = 1000 - ?$ Think $800 + 200 = 1000$ so $1000 - 200 = 800$

7. **True** $1000 - 90 = 900 + 10$

1000   900
$- 90$ $+ 10$
 910   910

Thousands	Hundreds	Tens	Ones
	9	10	
0	~~10~~		
~~1~~	~~0~~	~~0~~	0
−		9	0
	9	**1**	**0**

Hundreds	Tens	Ones
9	0	0
+	1	0
9	**1**	**0**

8. **True** $250 + 250$ $1000 - 500$
                  500      $=$ 500

Addition
Regrouping needed.
The 10 hundreds becomes 1000.

Hundreds	Tens	Ones
1		
2	5	0
2	5	0
+	~~10~~	0
	0	
5	**0**	**0**

$=$

Subtraction
Regrouping needed.
The 1000 becomes 10 hundreds

Thousands	Hundreds	Tens	Ones
0	10		
~~1~~	~~0~~	0	0
−	5	0	0
	5	**0**	**0**

9. **(A)**   422 $560 - 138 = 422$
You could decompose the numbers. Subtract the hundreds, then subtract the tens and ones. Then add those answers together. **5**60 − **1**38
                    $\mathbf{500} - \mathbf{1}00 = 400$
         and $60 - 38 = \underline{\ 22}$
                              422

10.　(C)　573　　　705 − 132 = 573　　or see

$$\begin{array}{r} {\scriptstyle 6\ 10} \\ \cancel{7}\ \cancel{0}\ 5 \\ -1\ 3\ 2 \\ \hline 5\ 7\ 3 \end{array}$$

Regrouping is needed here.

Measuring (2.MD.A.1, 2.MD.A.2), pages 114−115

1.　(A)　A ruler is best to measure the length of your foot.

2.　(D)　A measuring tape would be best to measure the length of the classroom.

3.　(C)　This rectangle is about 2 inches long.

4.　(B)　Jacob's dad could be 6 feet tall.

5.　(A)　A real car is about 18 feet long.

6.　Miles　Miles is the biggest unit.

7.　8　The bottle of water is about 8 inches tall using the ruler shown.

　　4　Half the bottle of water would be 4 inches tall.　4 + 4 = 8

　　2　If 4 people shared 8 inches of water they would each get 2 inches.

　　　2 + 2 + 2 + 2 = 8

　　　You could draw a picture or a chart to help you see the answer.

1 person	1	2	3	4	5	6	7	8

2 people	1	2	3	4	1	2	3	4

4 people	1	2	1	2	1	2	1	2

Person-1 will get 2 inches	Person-2 will get 2 inches	Person-3 will get 2 inches	Person-4 will get 2 inches

8.　Yes　They could both be correct.

　　　I know because 1 foot is 12 inches and if you change 4 feet into inches it would be

　　　12 + 12 + 12 + 12 = 40 + 8 = 48 inches.

　　　48 inches and 4 feet have the same length.

Measuring and Comparing (2.MD.A.3, 2.MD.A.4), pages 116−117

1.　(B)　3–4 centimeters

　　　Your shortest finger is about 3 to 4 centimeters long.

2.　(A)　8 inches　　　This paper is about 8 inches wide.

3.　(C)　6 inches　　　A new pencil is about 6 inches long.

4.　(D)　10 meters

　　　A meter is the longest measure. It is a little longer than a yard.

5.　(C)　about 9 cm long

　　　One paper clip measures about 3 centimeters long. The length of 3 paper clips together would be 3 + 3 + 3 or 9 centimeters long.

6. (A) 24 centimeters One apple could be about 8 centimeters long. The 3 apples would be 8 + 8 + 8 or 16 + 8 = 24 centimeters long.
The other choices are much too long.

7. 3 inches long

8. The father is taller. 3 feet 6 − 3 = 3

9. >6 Greater than 6. Actually, Ann would need about 9 of these little cat pictures to make a row across this sheet of paper.

Adding and Subtracting Lengths with Nancy (2.MD.B.5), pages 118–119

1. 8 18 − 10 = **8** inches left

2. 6 12 − 6 = **6** feet left

3. 15 The three tables would be 5 + 5 + 5 = **15** feet long

4. 72 36 inches + 36 inches = 30 + 30 + 6 + 6 =
60 + 12 = 60 + 10 + 2 = **72** inches

5. **Yes**, the two cars will fit in the driveway.
First I added the lengths of the two cars.
18 + 19 = 10 + 10 + 8 + 9 = 20 + 8 + 9 = 20 + 17 = **37** = length of 2 cars
Then I saw that the driveway measured 40 feet. 40 feet is longer than 37 feet, so I know the cars will fit.

6. 35 10 + 12 + 13 = 30 + 5 = **35** All together they are 35 units long.

7. **60** inches long in all
The first piece of wood: 18 + 18 = 20 + 16 = 36 inches
The second piece of wood: 12 + 12 = 20 + 4 = 24 inches
60 inches in all

8. Answers will vary. A 12-inch ruler is too short. It is much easier to use a long tape measure to measure something as large as the living room floor.

Numbers, Measuring, and Number Lines (2.MD.B.6), pages 120–123

1.

or, a student can draw a 6-unit line anywhere on the number line 1–10.

2. **Write** the numbers 1–9 to complete the number line below.

Show how you would represent 3 + 6 on the number line.

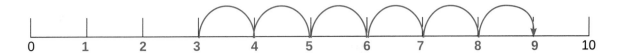

3 + 6 = **9** **Yes**, this matches what I drew on the number line.

3. **Write** the numbers 1–9 to complete the number line below.

Show how you would represent 8 – 2 on the number line above.

What is the difference between 8 and 2? **8 – 2 = 6**

If Trey had 8 markers and gave 2 markers to his sister, how many markers would he have left? He would have **6** markers left.

4. **Write** the numbers 71–79 to complete the number line below.

Show how you would represent 78 – 3 on the number line.

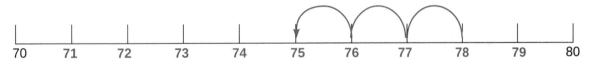

What is the difference between 78 and 3? **78 – 3 = 75**

Yes, this matches what I drew on the number line.

5. Use the number line below to teach a first grade student how to add 92 and 5 more.

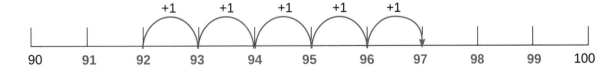

What is the sum of 92 and 5 more? **97**

6.

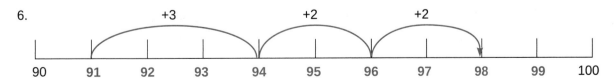

Write a number sentence that matches what this number line shows.

91 (+) 3 (+) 2 (+) 2 (=) 98

7.

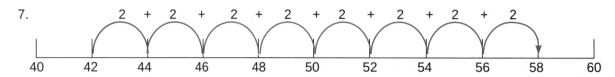

My father went shopping for grandpa's birthday gift. He had $58 and spent $42 on a shirt for grandpa.

Use the number line above to help you. (This number line counts by 2s.)

How much money did my father have left? **$16**

Did he have enough money to buy my mother a scarf for $15?

Yes. Explain how you know. 58 – 42 = 16. $16 is more than $15 so he has enough money to buy a scarf that costs $15.

8.

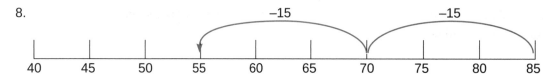

Write your own story about what this number line shows.

Use your own name in the story or some of your friends or family.

This number line counts by 5s. This shows 85 – 15 – 15 = 85 – 30 = 55

Answers will vary. Sample correct responses are listed below.

My name is Jennifer. I had 85 pennies and gave 30 to my sister. I still have 55 pennies left.

Or a student might write this as a question such as:

Jennifer had 85 pennies and gave 30 to her sister. How many pennies does Jennifer have now?

Working with Time and Money (2.MD.C.7, 2.MD.C.8), pages 124–127

1. (C)   7:00 A.M.

2. (C)   8:00 P.M.

3. (A)   7:05 A.M.

4. (B)   12:10 P.M.

5. (A)   two o'clock. The small hand points to the 2 and the big hand points to the 12. The small hand points to the "hour." The big hand points to the "minutes."

6. 8:15 A.M.   11:00 A.M.   12 Noon   3:30 P.M.   9:30 P.M.
   (A.M. are morning hours)   (P.M. are evening hours)

7. 5 hours. You can use a number line and count from 7 to 12.

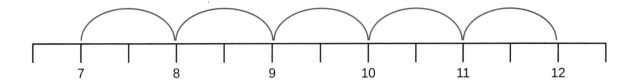

Or you can draw a clock and count on the clock.

8. **(B)** 5:30. The small hand is between the 5 and the 6 and the big hand points to the 6. The small hand points to the hour (which is halfway between 5 and 6) and the big hand points to the minutes (which is 30 minutes after 5).

9. Henrique is correct. The clock shows 15 minutes after one o'clock.
    I know because the small hand points to the hour and the large hand points to the minutes.
    Here, the small hand points to a little after 1 and the large hand points to 3 (which is at 15 minutes after 1:00).

10. **(B)** 32 cents   10 + 10 + 10 + 1 + 1 = 30 + 2 = 32

11. **(C)** 80 cents   25 + 25 + 10 + 10 + 10 = 50 + 30 = 80

12. **(D)** $8.50   8 dollars + 25 cents + 25 cents = $8.50

13. **(B)** $6.35   6 dollars + 10 + 10 + 10 + 5 = 6 dollars + 35 cents

14. Glenn   Glenn has 50 + 50 = 100 cents or $1.00
                  Tim has 25 + 20 + 8 = 53 cents

    47 cents   100 cents – 53 cents = 47 cents

15. quarters   It is easier to start with the coin with the largest value first.

    94 cents in all   50 + 30 + 10 + 4 = 90 + 4 = 94 cents

    Yes   35 cents + 40 cents = 75 cents
                  He has 94 cents, so he has more than 75 cents.

Line Plots, Charts, and Tally Marks (2.MD.D.9), pages 128–131

1. The 6 hearts on the right side.

2. The 4 ▢ and the 4 ☺ should be circled.

3. Cat 卌 + 卌 + || = 5 + 5 + 2 = 10 + 2 = 12

   Fish and Dog   They have the same number of tally marks. They each have 9 tally marks
   卌 + |||| = 5 + 4 = 9

   38   There are 38 pets listed in all.

Cat	卌 卌 ||	5 + 5	+ 2	= 12
Fish	卌 ||||	5	+ 4	= 9
Dog	卌 ||||	5	+ 4	= 9
Turtle	卌 |||	5	+ 3	= 8
				38

4. Grapes were chosen most often. 卌 + 卌 + ||| = 5 + 5 + 3 = 10 + 3 = 13

   Apples were chosen the fewest times. 卌 + ||| = 5 + 3 = 8

5. red   The red balloon was chosen the most often. It was chosen 9 times.

   6   Six students chose blue as their favorite balloon.

   22   There are 9 + 6 + 7 = 9 + 6 + 6 + 1 = 10 + 12 = 22 students in the class.

   No   There are 22 students in the class. Only 7 students chose yellow.

   Half of 22 is 11. See the diagram below. See 11 + 11 = 22.

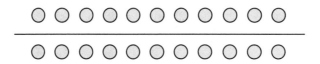

6. balls   Using the toys listed in the table, balls are the best kinds of toys to use outside.

   Any 2 of the following would be correct: pencils, crayons, paint, or chalk.

   3 different types. There are 3 different types of puzzles: farm, city, zoo.

7. 15   5 + 5 + 5 = 15 students ate fruit on Wednesday. (Remember, each X = 5.)

   Thursday (X = Only 5 students ate fruit on Thursday.)

   65   20 + 10 + 15 + 5 + 15 = 30 + 30 + 5 = 65 total.

   30   Monday = 5 + 5 + 5 + 5 and Tuesday = 5 + 5 = 10. 20 + 10 = 30 in all.

   85 students did **not** have fruit on Tuesday   95 – 10 = 85

8. They saved 20 nickels. (Remember, each X = 10.)

   They saved 30 cents. (Remember, each X = 10.) 10 + 10 + 10 = 30

   More pennies.   There are X + X + X = 10 + 10 + 10 = 30 pennies
                    There are X + X   = 10 + 10   = 20 quarters

1. **(D)**   A quadrilateral is a flat shape that has 4 sides.

2. **(A)**   A triangle has only three sides.

3. A **pentagon** has 5 sides and a **hexagon** has 6 sides.

4. **(B)**   A *pentagon* has exactly 5 sides and 5 angles.

5. **(C)**   A *pentagon.*

6. **(D)**   The hexagon has six angles.

7. You should have circled the [cube illustration] cube.

8. The cone looks like [cone illustration]. The ice cream *cone* and *cone* hat should be circled.

9. **Yes**   A box is often shaped like a [cube illustration] *cube.*

    Yes   The top of a desk looks like a ☐ *rectangle.*

    No   An apple is NOT shaped like a *cone.*

    No   Most television screens are NOT shaped like a *circle.*

    Most television screens are shaped like a ☐ *rectangle.*

    Yes   A ring has a *circle* ◯ shape.

10.

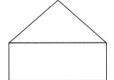

11.

12.

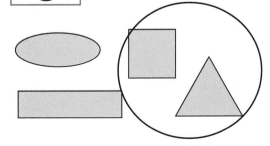

A face is a flat surface. The square has 4 equal sides or faces. The triangle has 3 equal sides or faces.

13.   **Yes**   Samantha is correct. A square is a 4-sided shape so it is also a *quadrilateral.*

1. (C)   21   See 3 rows with 7 squares in each row. 7 + 7 + 7 = 21
            or
            See 7 columns with 3 squares in each column.
            3 + 3 + 3 + 3 + 3 + 3 + 3 = 21

2. (B)   8

3. (B)   Four fourths

4. (B)   One half   2 fourths has the same value as one half

5. (C) $\frac{1}{4}$ The circle is divided into four parts. Each part = $\frac{1}{4}$ of the whole shape.

6. (A)   One half   One half + one half = one whole cupcake.

7. (A)   Thirds   The rectangle is divided into three equal parts.
                           Each part is one third of the whole.

8. three fourths or $\frac{3}{4}$ one whole = four fourths
                           four fourths – one fourth = three fourths

9. (A)   The pizza that is cut into fourths has larger pieces than the pizza that is cut into sixths.
           Look at the pictures below to see that this is true.

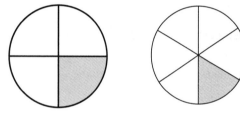

10. (D)   Four fifths of the freeway is not used as an express lane.
           Five fifths – one fifth = four fifths or 5 fifths – 1 fifth = 4 fifths

11. (C)   One third of the garden is left for other vegetables.
           Abigayle and her mother planted in 2 thirds of the garden. The whole garden is 3 thirds.
           3 thirds – 2 thirds = 1 third left.

12. (B)   One half of the chips were used, so there is still one half of the bag left for next time.
           One half + one half = one whole.

Math Practice Test

1. Count by fives and fill in the missing numbers.
   315, **320**, 325, **330**, 335, 340

2. Count by fives and fill in the missing numbers.
   175, **180**, 185, **190**, 195, 200

3. They drove **9** hours in all.

4. They drove **335** miles in all.
   90 + **45** + 200 = 90 + **10 + 35** + 200 =
   100 + 200 + 35 = 335

5. What is true about the number **562**?
   A. It is > 559.   Yes
   B. It has 5 ones.   No; it has 2 ones.
   C. It is an odd number.   No
   D. It is between 560 and 565. Yes
   E. It has six hundreds.   No; it has 6 tens.
   F. 562 + 8 = 570.   Yes

6. What is true about **427**?
   A. It is < 431.   Yes
   B. It has 2 tens.   Yes
   C. It is an even number.   No
   D. It is between 425 and 430. Yes
   E. It has seven hundreds.   No; it has 7 ones.
   F. 200 + 200 + 27 = 427.   Yes

7. 37   40 – 3 = 37

8. 14   20 – 3 – 3 = 20 – 6 = 14

9. 1:15 P.M.   15 minutes after one o'clock

10. 2:30 P.M.   30 minutes after two o'clock

11. 28 rolls all together.   12 + 16 = 28
    13 hot dogs were left   16 – 3 = 13

    ┌───┐
    │ 16 (–) 1 (–) 2 = 16 (–) 3 = 13   │
    └───┘

12. 20 pieces of fruit all together
    5 + 8 + 5 + 2 = 5 + 5 + 8 + 2 = 10 + 10 = 20
    17 pieces of fruit were left.   20 – 3 = 17

13.   27   17 + 10 = 27 windows in all.
                First floor: 12 + 2 + 3 = 17
                Second floor: 8 + 2 = 10 windows
      7   17 − 10 = 7

14.   82 windows in all   22 + 30 + 30 windows on the third floor.
      8 windows more   30 − 22 = 8

15.   Seat 133, 135, **137**, **139**, **141**, 143, 145, 147, **149**

16.   178 seats all together.   82 + 96 = 178

17.   210 students in the new school.
      45 + 55 + 50 + 60 = 100 + 110 = 210 students in the new school,
      15   60 − 45 = 15 more students in grade 3 than in grade 1.

18.   750   200 + 300 + 250 = 500 + 250 = 750
      875   750 + 125

      A sample correct reply might say:
      I know because I added 750 + 125 and saw that
            750 + 125 = 700 + 100 + 50 + 25 = 800 + 50 + 25 = 875

19.   Jeff and Jodi have the same amount of money.

20.   They each have 70 cents (or $ .70).

21.   Devon has the most money. He has 77 cents (or $.77)
      Brian has 10 + 10 + 10 + 2   = 32 cents
      Venice has 25 + 25   = 50 cents
      Marissa has 25 + 5   = 30 cents
      Jeff has 25 + 25 + 5 + 5 + 5 + 5   = 70 cents
      Jodi 10 + 10 + 10 + 10 + 10 + 10 + 10   = 70 cents
      Devon 25 + 25 + 25 + 2   = 77 cents

22 and 23. Answers to questions 22 and 23 vary based on student choices.

24.   50 + 70 + 90 = 210 cents or 2 dollars and 10 cents or $2.10

25.   240   582 − 342   To find the *difference* you *subtract.*

26.   30   53 − 23   To find the *difference* you *subtract.*

27.   150 + 28   is the *smallest* sum   146 + 36 = 182
                                                   150 + 28 = **178**
                                                   35 + 145 = 180

28.   123 + 48   is the *largest* sum   123 + 48 = **171**
                                                    32 + 129 = 161
                                                    134 + 27   = 161

29.   52 cards in all.   26 + 26 = 20 + 20 + 6 + 6 = 40 + 12 = 52
       40 cards did NOT have pictures on them.

       ┌───┐
       │   │
       │ I subtracted 12 from 52 and got 40.   │
       │ I wrote 52 – 12 = 40   │
       │   │
       └───┘

30.   92 beads in all   20 + 35 + 25 + 12
       20 + 30 + 20 + 10 + 0 + 5 + 5 + 2 = **80** + 12 = 92
       23 more white beads than pink beads 35 – 12 = 23

31.   a triangle   A triangle has only 3 sides and 3 angles.

32.   a square   A square has 4 sides and 4 angles.

33.   This line measures about **6** inches long.

34.   This piece of paper is about **11** inches tall.

35.   This shape should be circled.

36.   **(C)**   One third or $\frac{1}{3}$ of the circle is shaded.

37.   **(C)**   One half or $\frac{1}{2}$ of the candy bar is left.

38.   Various answers are correct. The student should shade in $\frac{1}{4}$ of the rectangle. As long as the
       student shades in 3 of the smaller rectangles the answer is correct. Sample correct answers are
       shown below.

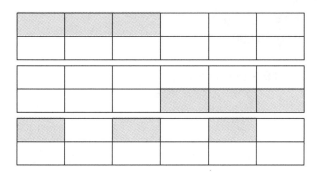

Juan and Marissa Go Shopping

39. $8 or 8   Four pair of socks cost $8.

40. $2 or 2   2 + 2 + 2 + 2 = 8   If four pairs of socks cost $8, then one pair costs $2.

$1	$2	$3	$4	$5	$6	$7	$8
$2		$2		$2		$2	
1 pair of socks		1 pair of socks		1 pair of socks		1 pair of socks	

41. $17 or 17 dollars
       Juan's shoes cost   25.00
       Marissa's socks cost   − 8.00   Subtract to find the difference.
                                  17.00

42. $29   20 (+)   6   (+)   3   = 29 or $29

       vitamins (+) cards (+) bubbles = total

A New Pet

43.   **22** (+) **10** (+) **12** = 20 + 10 + 10 + 2 + 0 + 2 = 40 + 4 = **44** fish all together.

44.   **The big black dog** had the most puppies. 8 is bigger than 5.

45.   She had **3** more puppies than the poodle dog.
       8 − 5 = 3

46.   **$95**   80 + 15 = 80 + 10 + 5 = 90 + 5 = 95

47.   **$4.50** or **4 dollars and 50 cents**
       1 can of puppy food = 50 cents,
       5 cans cost 50 + 50 + 50 + 50 + 50 = 100 + 100 + 50 = 250
       250 cents or 2 dollars and 50 cents or $2.50
       1 box of cookie bones cost 2 dollars
       $2 and 50 cents + $2 = 4 dollars and 50 cents or $4.50

48.   **5:00**   2 + 3 = 5

49.   **58** pounds
       8 (+) 25 (+) 25 = 58 pounds.

50.   (C)   **a large bag of apples**

APPENDIX A

ENGLISH LANGUAGE ARTS
COMMON CORE STANDARDS

Reading: Literature
CCSS.ELA-Literacy.RL.2.1 Ask and answer such questions as *who, what, where, when, why, and how* to demonstrate understanding of key details in a text.
CCSS.ELA-Literacy.RL.2.2 Recount stories, including fables and folktales from diverse cultures, and determine the central message, lesson, or moral.
CCSS.ELA-Literacy.RL.2.3 Describe how characters in a story respond to major events and challenges.
CCSS.ELA-Literacy.RL.2.4 Describe how words and phrases (e.g., regular beats, alliteration, rhymes, repeated lines) supply rhythm and meaning in a story, poem, or song.
CCSS.ELA-Literacy.RL.2.5 Describe the overall structure of a story, including describing how the beginning introduces the story and the ending concludes the action.
CCSS.ELA-Literacy.RL.2.6 Acknowledge differences in the points of view of characters, including by speaking in a different voice for each character when reading dialogue aloud.
CCSS.ELA-Literacy.RL.2.7 Use information gained from the illustrations and words in a print or digital text to demonstrate understanding of its characters, setting, or plot.
CCSS.ELA-Literacy.RL.2.9 Compare and contrast two or more versions of the same story (e.g., Cinderella stories) by different authors or from different countries.
CCSS.ELA-Literacy.RL.2.10 By the end of the year, read and comprehend literature, including stories and poetry in the grades 2–3 text complexity band proficiently with scaffolding as needed at the high end of the range.
Reading: Informational Text
CCSS.ELA-Literacy.RI.2.1 Ask and answer such questions as *who, what, where, when, why, and how* to demonstrate understanding of key details in a text.
CCSS.ELA-Literacy.RI.2.2 Identify the main topic of a multi-paragraph text as well as the focus of specific paragraphs within the text.
CCSS.ELA-Literacy.RI.2.3 Describe the connection between a series of historical events, scientific ideas or concepts, or steps in technical procedures in a text.
CCSS.ELA-Literacy.RI.2.4 Determine the meaning of words and phrases in a text relevant to a *grade 2 topic or subject area*.
CCSS.ELA-Literacy.RI.2.5 Know and use text features (e.g., captions, bold print, subheadings, glossaries, indexes, electronic menus, icons) to locate key facts or information in a text efficiently.
CCSS.ELA-Literacy.RI.2.6 Identify the main purpose of a text, including what the author wants to answer, explain, or describe.
CCSS.ELA-Literacy.RI.2.7 Explain how specific images (e.g., a diagram showing how a machine works) contribute to and clarify a text.
CCSS.ELA-Literacy.RI.2.8 Describe how reasons support specific points the author makes in a text.
CCSS.ELA-Literacy.RI.2.9 Compare and contrast the most important points presented by two texts on the same topic.

CCSS.ELA-Literacy.RI.2.10 By the end of the year, read and comprehend informational texts, including history/social studies, science, and technical texts, in the grades 2–3 text complexity band proficiently with scaffolding as needed at the high end of the range.

Reading: Foundational Skills

CCSS.ELA-Literacy.RF.2.3 Know and apply grade-level phonics and word analysis skills in decoding words. (a, b, c, and f)

CCSS.ELA-Literacy.RF.2.4 Read with sufficient accuracy and fluency to support comprehension. (a, b, and c)

Writing

CCSS.ELA-Literacy.W.2.1 Write opinion pieces in which they introduce the topic or book they are writing about, state an opinion, supply reasons that support the opinion, use linking words (e.g., because, and, also) to connect opinion and reasons, and provide a concluding statement or section.

CCSS.ELA-Literacy.W.2.2 Write informative/explanatory texts in which they introduce a topic, use facts and definitions to develop points, and provide a concluding statement or section.

CCSS.ELA-Literacy.W.2.3 Write narratives to develop real or imagined experiences or events using effective technique, descriptive details, and clear event sequences.

CCSS.ELA-Literacy.W.2.5 With guidance and support from adults and peers, focus on a topic and strengthen writing as needed by revising and editing.

CCSS.ELA-Literacy.W.2.6 With guidance and support from peers and adults, use a variety of digital tools to produce and publish writing, including in collaboration with peers.

CCSS.ELA-LITERACY.CCRA.W.4 (Anchor Standard) Produce clear and coherent writing in which the development, organization, and style are appropriate to task, purpose, and audience

CCSS.ELA-Literacy.W.3.7 Conduct short research projects that build knowledge about a topic.

CCSS.ELA-Literacy.W.3.8 Recall information from experiences or gather information from print and digital sources; take brief notes on sources and sort evidence into provided categories.

CCSS.ELA-Literacy.W.3.10 Write routinely over extended time frames (time for research, reflection, and revision) and shorter time frames (a single sitting or a day or two) for a range of discipline-specific tasks, purposes, and audiences.

Speaking and Listening

CCSS.ELA-Literacy.SL.2.1 Participate in collaborative discussions with diverse partners about *grade 2 topics and texts*, with peers and adults in smaller and larger groups. (a, b, c)

CCSS.ELA-Literacy.SL.2.2 Recount key ideas or details from a text read aloud or information presented orally or through other media.

CCSS.ELA-Literacy.SL.2.3 Ask and answer questions about information about what a speaker says in order to clarify comprehension, gather additional information, or deepen understanding of a topic or issue.

CCSS.ELA-Literacy.SL.2.4 Tell a story or recount an experience with appropriate facts and relevant, descriptive details, speaking audibly in coherent sentences.

CCSS.ELA-Literacy.SL.2.5 Create audio recordings of stories or poems; add drawings or other visual displays to stories or recounts of experiences when appropriate to clarify ideas, thoughts, and feelings.

CCSS.ELA-Literacy.SL.2.6 Produce complete sentences when appropriate to task and situation in order to provide requested detail or clarification.

Language
CCSS.ELA-Literacy.L.2.1 Demonstrate command of the conventions of standard English grammar and usage when writing or speaking.
CCSS.ELA-Literacy.L.2.1.A Use collective nouns (e.g., group)
CCSS.ELA-Literacy.L.2.1.B Form and use frequently occurring irregular plural nouns (e.g., feet, children, teeth, mice, fish).
CCSS.ELA-Literacy.L.2.1.C Use reflexive pronouns (e.g., myself, ourselves).
CCSS.ELA-Literacy.L.2.1.D Form and use the past tense of frequently occurring irregular verbs (e.g., sat, hid, told).
CCSS.ELA-Literacy.L.2.1.E Use adjectives and adverbs, and choose between them depending on what is to be modified.
CCSS.ELA-Literacy.L.2.1.F Produce, expand, and rearrange complete, simple, and compound sentences (e.g., *The boy watched the movie; The little boy* watched the movie; The action movie was watched by the little boy).
CCSS.ELA-Literacy.L.2.2 Demonstrate command of the conventions of standard English capitalization, punctuation, and spelling when writing.
CCSS.ELA-Literacy.L.2.2.A Capitalize holidays, product names, and geographic names.
CCSS.ELA-Literacy.L.2.2.B Use an apostrophe to form contractions and frequently occurring possessives.
CCSS.ELA-Literacy.L.2.2.D Generalize learned spelling patterns when writing words (e.g., cage>>badge; boy>>boil).
CCSS.ELA-Literacy.L.2.3 Use knowledge of language and its conventions when writing, speaking, reading, or listening. A. Compare formal and informal uses of English.
CCSS.ELA-Literacy.L.2.4 Determine or clarify the meaning of unknown and multiple-meaning words and phrases based on grade 2 reading and content, choosing flexibly from an array of strategies.
CCSS.ELA-Literacy.L.2.4.A Use sentence-level context as a clue to the meaning of a word or phrase.
CCSS.ELA-Literacy.L.2.4.B Determine the meaning of the new word formed when a known prefix is added to a known word (e.g., happy/unhappy, tell/retell).
CCSS.ELA-Literacy.L.2.4.C Use a known root word as a clue to the meaning of an unknown word with the same root (e.g., addition, additional).
CCSS.ELA-Literacy.L.2.4.D Use knowledge of the meaning of individual words to predict the meaning of compound words (e.g., birdhouse, lighthouse, housefly; bookshelf, notebook, bookmark).
CCSS.ELA-Literacy.L.2.4.E Use glossaries and beginning dictionaries, both print and digital, to determine or clarify the meaning of words and phrases.
CCSS.ELA-Literacy.L.2.5 Demonstrate understanding of figurative language, word relationships, and nuances in word meanings.
CCSS.ELA-Literacy.L.2.5.A Identify real-life connections between words and their use (e.g., describe foods that are spicy or juicy).
CCSS.ELA-Literacy.L.2.5.B Distinguish shades of meaning among closely related verbs (e.g., toss, throw, hurl) and closely related adjectives (e.g., thin, slender, skinny, scrawny).
CCSS.ELA-Literacy.L.2.6 Use words and phrases acquired through conversations, reading and being read to, and responding to texts, including using adjectives and adverbs to describe (e.g., When other kids are happy that makes me happy).

MATH COMMON CORE STANDARDS

Operations and Algebraic Thinking
Represent and solve problems involving addition and subtraction.
CCSS.Math.Content.2.OA.A.1 Use addition and subtraction within 100 to solve one- and two-step word problems involving situations of adding to, taking from, putting together, taking apart, and comparing, with unknowns in all positions, e.g., by using drawings and equations with a symbol for the unknown number to represent the problem.
Add and subtract within 20.
CCSS.Math.Content.2.OA.B.2 Fluently add and subtract within 20 using mental strategies. By end of grade 2, know from memory all sums of two one-digit numbers.
Work with equal groups of objects to gain foundations for multiplication.
CCSS.Math.Content.2.OA.C.3 Determine whether a group of objects (up to 20) has an odd or even number of members, e.g., by pairing objects or counting them by 2s; write an equation to express an even number as a sum of two equal addends.
CCSS.Math.Content.2.OA.C.4 Use addition to find the total number of objects arranged in rectangular arrays with up to 5 rows and up to 5 columns; write an equation to express the total as a sum of equal addends.

Number and Operations in Base Ten
Understand place value.
CCSS.Math.Content.2.NBT.A.1 Understand that the three digits of a three-digit number represent amounts of hundreds, tens, and ones; e.g., 706 equals 7 hundreds, 0 tens, and 6 ones. Understand the following as special cases:
CCSS.Math.Content.2.NBT.A.1 (a) 100 can be thought of as a bundle of ten tens—called a "hundred."
CCSS.Math.Content.2.NBT.A.1 (b) The numbers 100, 200, 300, 400, 500, 600, 700, 800, 900 refer to one, two, three, four, five, six, seven, eight, or nine hundreds (and 0 tens and 0 ones).
CCSS.Math.Content.2.NBT.A.2 Count within 1000; skip-count by 5s, 10s, and 100s.
CCSS.Math.Content.2.NBT.A.3 Read and write numbers to 1000 using base-ten numerals, number names, and expanded form.
CCSS.Math.Content.2.NBT.A.4 Compare two three-digit numbers based on meanings of the hundreds, tens, and ones digits, using >, =, and < symbols to record the results of comparisons.
Use place value understanding and properties of operations to add and subtract.
CCSS.Math.Content.2.NBT.B.5 Fluently add and subtract within 100 using strategies based on place value, properties of operations, and/or the relationship between addition and subtraction.
CCSS.Math.Content.2.NBT.B.6 Add up to four two-digit numbers using strategies based on place value and properties of operations.
CCSS.Math.Content.2.NBT.B.7 Add and subtract within 1000, using concrete models or drawings and strategies based on place value, properties of operations, and/or the relationship between addition and subtraction; relate the strategy to a written method. Understand that in adding or subtracting three-digit numbers, one adds or subtracts hundreds and hundreds, tens and tens, ones and ones; and sometimes it is necessary to compose or decompose tens or hundreds.

CCSS.Math.Content.2.NBT.B.8 Mentally add 10 or 100 to a given number 100–900, and mentally subtract 10 or 100 from a given number 100–900.

CCSS.Math.Content.2.NBT.B.9 Explain why addition and subtraction strategies work, using place value and the properties of operations.

Measurement & Data

Measure and estimate lengths in standard units.

CCSS.Math.Content.2.MD.A.1 Measure the length of an object by selecting and using appropriate tools such as rulers, yardsticks, meter sticks, and measuring tapes.

CCSS.Math.Content.2.MD.A.2 Measure the length of an object twice, using length units of different lengths for the two measurements; describe how the two measurements relate to the size of the unit chosen.

CCSS.Math.Content.2.MD.A.3 Estimate lengths using units of inches, feet, centimeters, and meters.

CCSS.Math.Content.2.MD.A.4 Measure to determine how much longer one object is than another, expressing the length difference in terms of a standard length unit.

Relate addition and subtraction to length.

CCSS.Math.Content.2.MD.B.5 Use addition and subtraction within 100 to solve word problems involving lengths that are given in the same units, e.g., by using drawings (such as drawings of rulers) and equations with a symbol for the unknown number to represent the problem.

CCSS.Math.Content.2.MD.B.6 Represent whole numbers as lengths from 0 on a number-line diagram with equally spaced points corresponding to the numbers 0, 1, 2, ..., and represent whole-number sums and differences within 100 on a number-line diagram.

Work with time and money.

CCSS.Math.Content.2.MD.C.7 Tell and write time from analog and digital clocks to the nearest five minutes, using a.m. and p.m.

CCSS.Math.Content.2.MD.C.8 Solve word problems involving dollar bills, quarters, dimes, nickels, and pennies, using $ and ¢ symbols appropriately. Example: If you have 2 dimes and 3 pennies, how many cents do you have?

Represent and interpret data.

CCSS.Math.Content.2.MD.D.9 Generate measurement data by measuring lengths of several objects to the nearest whole unit, or by making repeated measurements of the same object. Show the measurements by making a line plot, where the horizontal scale is marked off in whole-number units.

CCSS.Math.Content.2.MD.D.10 Draw a picture graph and a bar graph (with single-unit scale) to represent a data set with up to four categories. Solve simple put-together, take-apart, and compare problems using information presented in a bar graph.

Geometry

Reason with shapes and their attributes.

CCSS.Math.Content.2.G.A.1 Recognize and draw shapes having specified attributes, such as a given number of angles or a given number of equal faces. Identify triangles, quadrilaterals, pentagons, hexagons, and cubes.

CCSS.Math.Content.2.G.A.2 Partition a rectangle into rows and columns of same-size squares and count to find the total number of them.

CCSS.Math.Content.2.G.A.3 Partition circles and rectangles into two, three, or four equal shares, describe the shares using the words halves, thirds, half of, a third of, etc., and describe the whole as two halves, three thirds, four fourths. Recognize that equal shares of identical wholes need not have the same shape.

APPENDIX B
SIMPLE WRITING RUBRIC

Use the lists below to check your writing for standards (2.W.1) Write Your Opinion, (2.W.2) Writing Explanatory Texts, and (2.W.3) Writing Narrative Texts.

List A: This list is for all writing, standards 2.W.1–3. You can check off each one while checking your writing.

- ✔ Capitalization: Proper nouns and sentences should begin with a capital letter.
- ✔ Organization: The writing is in paragraph form and follows an understandable order.
- ✔ Punctuation: Every sentence ends with a period, question mark, or exclamation point.
- ✔ Spelling: Most of the words are spelled correctly.

List B: Use list A plus this list to help check your writing when you write your opinion.

- ✔ My details are complete, factual, and convincing.
- ✔ My readers understand how I feel about my topic.

List C: Use List A plus this list to help check your writing when you write explanatory texts.

- ✔ My details teach something and answer reader's questions.

List D: Use List A plus this list to help check your writing when you write narrative texts.

- ✔ My details use the five senses (looks, feels, tastes, smells, sounds).
- ✔ My writing describes character(s), setting, and plot.